VENICE

VENICE

A Century on the Gulf

LARRY R. HUMES

Foreword by Harry Klinkhamer

THE
History
PRESS

Published by The History Press
Charleston, SC
www.historypress.com

Copyright © 2025 by Larry R. Humes

Cover photos courtesy of Venice Historical Resources and Liesl Walsh.

All rights reserved

First published 2025

Manufactured in the United States

ISBN 9781467159548

Library of Congress Control Number: 2024950547

I dedicate this book to our granddaughter, Caroline May Pittius, in hopes she will one day experience the joy and knowledge of understanding what has come before. Our past is what illumines our path to the future.

CONTENTS

Contents

FOREWORD

I first met Larry Humes in late 2017. It was about a month after taking my position of historical resources manager with the City of Venice. He and another individual invited me to his office to discuss the possibility of relocating the Venice Museum to a larger space with financial support from donors. That project never materialized, but right away I learned three things about Larry: his passion for Venice history, his talent as a storyteller and his unflagging ability to come up with interesting ideas. None of this should come as a surprise seeing that he was an alumnus of the Kentucky Military Institute (you'll read about it in this book) and had a long career in public relations and communication.

So, with Venice's centennial approaching in the distance, I decided to turn the tables on Larry. This time *I* came up with the interesting idea: it was time we had a new history of Venice published, and Larry was just the person to write it. Venice is a community with a great interest—if not passion—in its history. Larry has fed that interest regularly with his contributions on local history to the *Venice Gondolier* newspaper. He has written about historic neighborhoods, interviewed old-timers and researched past events—all for the same goal of telling stories about the city's past.

Venice is not a huge place, but it does have a very unique and interesting history. So much so that not one but two publications document the city's past. Plus, several other booklets and publications compile memories from individuals or groups. With all that written about Venice, there was still a need for Larry and this book. Larry's prose makes this a page-turner, sharing with all of you the stories about the people and places that make up this city. This is in contrast to previously published works that either serve more as reference or cover the very basics. The goal here was to hit that sweet spot in between those two.

Although some might quip about the early history not being included here, this work is coming out in time for when the Venice we know now—south of Roberts Bay and becoming incorporated—is turning one hundred. There is enough in the early chapters to provide the foundation of what would become the town of Venice. Probably more importantly, Larry has pushed the boundaries of what is part of Venice history. By shifting forward and away from the late nineteenth and early twentieth centuries, you can now read about the Venice Army Air Base, Ringling Bros. and Barnum & Bailey Circus, the Intracoastal and 9/11. Related to most of that is the growth of Venice in the post–World War II era that far exceeded what happened in the 1920s.

The people, the events and the stories told within these pages show how luck, fate and serendipity should have us rethinking being the "City on the Gulf" to instead being the "City of Nine Lives." The way the Brotherhood of Locomotive Engineers (BLE) was late to the Florida Land Boom and bet so heavily on this investment gamble, Venice was pretty much set up for failure. And yet we are celebrating a century. This is in no small part to those early Venetians who bought and lived here after the BLE pulled out. It is also due to that unfortunate fire on Florida's east coast that destroyed the Kentucky Military Institute's winter campus. And that telegram sent by Finn Casperson. And also that disagreement between the City of Sarasota and the circus—one we would unfortunately repeat. Venice thrives because of all these things, but the underlying foundation for the city's longevity and popularity has to do with one gentleman who never lived here: John Nolen.

Nolen was a pioneer in the practice of city planning. He became a progressive during a time historians call the Progressive era. It was when people thought that government could do good to benefit society because it had the means and motivation to do so. As Larry writes, "Nolen believed Venice, like every city, should be a dramatic, aesthetic experience. And it should be available to all its residents, regardless of their cultural or economic status." The blank slate that was Venice offered Nolen the opportunity to design a community of his vision with a seemingly endless supply of BLE money and enthusiasm to make it happen. When that money and enthusiasm dried up, it left Nolen financially battered and his plan complete on paper but not in real life. This would leave Venice unfinished and on its own moving forward. Larry writes, "By 1930, the City of Venice was badly bruised, but still in the proverbial ring." It meant that the priority was keeping the streetlights on rather than continuing with Nolen's Plan. In a way, that proved beneficial to Venice. It meant that the city was ignored, which led to "preservation by neglect." There was no reason to tear down the historic fabric of Venice because there was not a strong demand then to develop the city.

It would not be until more prosperous times that Venice would revisit maintaining Nolen's Plan. By then, changes in city growth and architectural styles had occurred. What had been planned for farms now became subdivisions as the city outgrew his plan. But the city's interest in Nolen's work grew and would be evoked in comprehensive plans, the creation of a new architectural review board and, ultimately, a National Historic District recognizing his plan. In fact, like Abraham Lincoln in Congress, John Nolen's name has been mentioned over and over at Venice City Council meetings from all over the development spectrum. In every instance, speakers would claim to answer the question "WWJD— What Would John Do?" For much of the past one hundred years, the City of Venice has tried to answer that question. Would Nolen build the Intracoastal Waterway? Would he build an airport south of the city? Would he plan gated communities?

Larry goes on to share the stories of some of those previously mentioned "nine lives" Venice had from Dr. Fred Albee, Colonel Charles B. Richmond, Bud Wimmers, Arthur Concello and others who kept the city going. Along with Nolen's plan, these stories are part of Venice's charm. But that charm can also be reflected in the names of Venice's bridges, the works of art sculpted by Victor Lundy and Ralph Twitchell and the mission of city government to keep Venice—among other things—historic.

It is fascinating how Venice benefited from so many institutions that would call Venice home. Typically, a community would be proud to brag about a school, military base or business that positively affected them. But here, it would be all those and more. It begs the question, "What else could put Venice on the map?" Unfortunately, it is not always something positive. Terrorism and unbridled growth would be highlights (or lowlights?) of the beginning of the twenty-first century. If anything, it goes to show that Venice is not always perfect and ideal. What community is? History should not be seen through rose-colored glasses. And so, we still love Venice just the same.

As I started out saying, Larry has a knack for telling stories and loves Venice history. What better combination could there be to author a book such as this? I'm not sure. Perhaps we need to wait another one hundred years to find out. In the meantime, enjoy reading *Venice: A Century on the Gulf*. It has been a pleasure to be a part of its creation, and I am excited to see what new stories emerge about Venice history.

HARRY KLINKHAMER
Historical Resources Manager
February 2024

ACKNOWLEDGEMENTS

Many hands provided support in the creation of this book, and to each of them, I am forever grateful.

Harry Klinkhamer, who serves as manager of Venice's Division of Historical Resources and was kind enough to write the foreword, first suggested the idea for this book and has offered suggestions and his editing skills throughout the process. Harry also selected the photos that were used throughout. I could not have written this book, Harry, without your help.

My thanks to Jon Watson, curator and collections manager of the more than thirty thousand objects in the city's Julia Cousins Laning and Dale Laning Archives & Research Center (CLARC), who is always there with a needed photo or historical detail when I'm on a deadline (too often).

Clarke Pressley, past president of the Venice Area Historical Society and research volunteer at the CLARC. Clarke, you have always been my go-to source for anything involving local history. I would be too intimidated to publish without your stamp of approval.

My thanks to the editorial staff of the *Venice Gondolier* newspaper, who graciously allowed me to be an unofficial member of your team. And my special thanks to reporters Kim Cool and Bob Mudge, who shared their knowledge with me about those chapters that dealt with the Ringling Circus in Venice and the city's involvement with 9/11. Having worked in and around journalism for more than four decades, I value most the time working with all you professionals.

Liesl Walsh, I fell in love with your photographs at first sight. Your images speak more than my words ever could. I especially thank you for allowing us to use your photograph of the historic train depot on the cover of this book.

I am grateful for all those writers and historians who paved the way in documenting Venice history—particularly Frank Cassell, Janet Snyder-Matthews, Jeff LaHurd, Dorothy Korwek, Gregg Turner, George Youngberg Sr. and W. Earl Aumann. I stand on your shoulders.

And finally, my special thanks to my life partner and editor-in-chief. Carol Humes not only encouraged me to take on this assignment, but she also proofread and offered suggestions throughout the past sixteen months. I depend on you far more than you will ever know.

THE PROMOTER

A few dozen settlers during the latter half of the nineteenth century managed to eke out a living amid the pine barrens and palmetto scrub along Florida's west coast. It took a native New Englander and entrepreneur, however, to realize the potential for developing the frontier that eventually would become known as the Suncoast.

Joseph Haley Lord at one time owned more than seventy thousand acres of land, making him the largest landowner in the region. He was instrumental in transforming Sarasota from a small fishing town to a modern city. And perhaps most importantly, he was the biggest promoter of the area, attracting people of means from all over to invest in the area's growth.

Lord was born on December 8, 1860, in the small coastal city of Wells in southern Maine. The son of Stillman and Emily Lord and one of nine children, he grew up on the family's farm and helped with his share of chores. He would later declare that the first dollar he ever earned was picking blueberries among the rocks of New England. "I was only a shaver of seven or eight when I did this," he said, "and up to that time I had not had a real suit of store-bought clothes. I continued the picking until I had saved up enough to buy one." Lord added that Sunday did not come often enough, as it was the only day of the week he was allowed to wear the suit.

Lord attended Brown University, where, thanks to his passion for great literature and his aptitude for composition, he served for a time as chair of the English Department. He earned his law degree from Brown in 1885 and married Franc Mabel Webber on August 23 of that year.

Francie, as she was called by friends and family, was the daughter of Frank and Sarah Webber and was born in St. Albans, Maine, on August 28, 1862. Her family started visiting the Orlando area during the early 1880s, and Frank Webber began purchasing Orange County property there in 1884. He and Sarah deeded several parcels of land to Franc the following year when she was twenty-two years old and still single. She began purchasing additional real estate all over the county, eventually owning nearly fifty acres.

Lord briefly practiced law in Sioux Falls, South Dakota, and Chicago before the couple relocated to Orlando, where he was admitted to the Florida Bar on May 20, 1886. He also purchased a small citrus orchard there and planned to invest in the growing business of phosphate mining. He was still practicing law, however. The *Orange County Gazetteer* of 1887 listed Frank Webber as an orange grower and Lord as an attorney.

A great freeze in 1885–86 sent temperatures plummeting, destroying much of the citrus crop. The Lords packed up their possessions and moved to a hopefully more hospitable climate on Florida's southwest coast. Franc's mother, by then a widow, would follow the couple to the Sarasota-Bradenton area, arriving in 1897.

Lord began acquiring land throughout the southern part of Manatee County while establishing citrus groves in Bee Ridge and a ninety-acre grove on the southern bank of the Bay of Venice (today's Roberts Bay).

In addition to his interest in growing citrus, Lord pursued other business ventures, such as operating a fleet of fishing boats along the coast. On March 10, 1893, just a decade after phosphate mining began in Florida, he formed a partnership with O.L. Geer, Edward Records and L.M. Simpson with the intent of mining phosphate on 9,790 acres of land on and near Venice Bay. To finance the operation, they jointly formed a stock company with the intent of selling 100,000 shares of stock at a par value of ten dollars per share.

They would use the $1 million in revenue generated to purchase the needed land from Lord and establish a factory for extracting the phosphate. The venture apparently never materialized.

In 1896, Lord built a two-story Queen Anne/Victorian-style house in the middle of his Bay of Venice citrus grove. With four rooms on each floor and a wrap-around porch that featured large, double-hung windows designed to mitigate the hot and humid summers, it was an ideal house for raising a growing family. Their daughter, Louise, was born in 1887, with son Joseph Jr. born ten years later. The Lords lived in the house until about 1903, at which time they took up residence in Sarasota. George Higel and his family occupied the house beginning in 1910 after Lord hired him to manage the grove.

Joseph Lord House, circa 1940. *Venice Historical Resources.*

With the arrival of the railroad in Sarasota in 1903, Lord focused his attention on transforming that small coastal city. By 1904, he owned four of the five corners at Five Points, considered the hub of downtown Sarasota, and eventually owned more than two hundred lots throughout the city. One of his first acquisitions was the Sarasota House hotel on the corner of Main Street and Central Avenue.

In addition to purchasing land, he also encouraged improvements in the city. For example, when citizens complained about the stench from open sewers, he replaced them with six-inch sewage pipes that ran from his hotel property to Sarasota Bay. Neighboring businesses could then tap into the drainage pipes for a small fee.

Lord became one of the biggest promoters of life on the Suncoast. Maintaining an office in the Scollay Building in Boston, he boasted in a flyer the many advantages of living in a tropical paradise: "Florida is the nation's asset....Its salubrious climate is the most perfect on the continent. It is the nation's best playground, health, and recreation resort. It is a great out-of-doors sanatorium, where people live in the open the year round and breathe its sun-soaked, salt-laden air."

Claiming that Florida was the country's mid-winter fruit and market garden, Lord stated that the area was shipping up north, chiefly through the winter months, eighty thousand car loads of fruits, vegetables and other products, valued at $150 million. He added that the tourism trade already amounted to $30 million annually.

On the back of a postcard mailed to prospective investors, he penned a humorous poem to entice those trapped in northern winter weather to consider relocating to sunny Florida:

> *Would you like to settle down*
> *In a sunny southern town,*
> *Far away from all the care and strife and woe?*
> *Would you like to live a dream*
> *And have lots of milk and cream,*
> *From your own contented cows, who'd smile at you?*

Would you like to raise some chickens
That would lay eggs like the Dickens,
Until you'd scarcely think it could be true?
Would you like some orange trees
In a place they never freeze,
And luscious grapefruit ripening at your door?
Down in nature's paradise,
Where there's never snow or ice,
And the gentle breezes whisper evermore.
Would you like to have your health,
And a sure amount of wealth
Always coming in to make your heart feel glad?
Where the problems of today
Are just lightly cast away,
And you never have to think of feeling sad?
If these things appeal to you,
Let me tell you what to do,
Take a postcard and sit down and write to me.
I've a booklet here for you,
Every word of which is true,
And I'll send it to you absolutely free.
Now's the time to make a hit,
So you just pack up your kit,
And take advantage while the price is low,
For in all the world today,
There is just one place to stay,
It is SARASOTA where you want to go.

He formed a real estate business with Arthur B. Edwards, Sarasota's first elected mayor, and together they opened an office in Chicago's historic Marquette Building to promote business opportunities in the Sarasota area.

During the winter of 1910, Lord ran an advertisement in the *Chicago Daily Tribune*, citing many benefits of living and investing in the Suncoast. "I am one of the largest growers and landowners in Manatee County and can furnish you with any kind or size of property desired," he went on to state. "I also improve lands and raise groves for purchasers."

As it turned out, wealthy Chicago socialite Bertha Honoré Palmer's father, H.H. Honoré, also maintained an office in the Marquette Building.

Joseph H. Lord. *Venice Historical Resources.*

She encouraged him to stop by Lord's Chicago office and get more information on the Gulf Coast.

Palmer would become a prime investor on the Suncoast and would purchase much of Lord's real estate holdings. Together, they would form the Sarasota-Venice Land Company, with Lord serving as vice-president of the company, and would maintain offices not only in Sarasota but also in Evanston, Illinois, where the Lords would spend their summer months.

In 1916, Lord pumped new life into the city's board of trade, precursor to Sarasota's chamber of commerce, and served as its president for the next two years. One project taken on by the board was the printing of ten thousand copies of a booklet touting the city's many advantages. Lord, Owen Burns and Adrian Honoré, Bertha's brother, donated funds to help pay the cost of printing.

As president of the board of trade, Lord was an advocate for the growing movement for the city of Sarasota and all lands south of it to secede from Manatee County. Sarasota County was formed on May 14, 1921, and Florida Governor Cary Hardee appointed Lord to serve as the county's first state representative in Tallahassee.

"J.H. Lord is one of the biggest and jolliest men in the State," wrote one journalist. "Mr. Lord is, indeed, a big fellow; big and brawny; big ideas and bigger purposes than the mere political climber; a man of wealth and of powerful physique, endowed with business grit and a splendid personal impressionableness. Says he is a booster for the whole State of Florida and he is."

Along with community leaders, Lord realized that good transportation was necessary if Florida's west coast was going to thrive. The area was mostly navigable by water, and the Seaboard Airline Railroad extended a spur from Sarasota to Venice in 1911. Roads south of Sarasota, however, were still primitive, and many consisted of little more than ruts in the sand. Having lived the majority of his life in the days of the horse and buggy, Lord was attempting to teach himself to drive along those undeveloped paths. An article in a 1913 edition of the *Sarasota Times* marked his progress: "He already has [his automobile] educated so that it will do anything but climb trees, and it will get that habit under his tutorship."

In September 1922, Lord joined forty-six other Sarasota leaders and their wives on a weeklong motorcade to eleven Florida cities to "get better acquainted with other towns in Florida and gain first-hand knowledge of city improvements which would be of material benefit to Sarasota."

Lord embarked on perhaps his largest project in the early 1920s, when Florida was experiencing a land boom. He demolished the old Sarasota House hotel and replaced it with the city's first "skyscraper," the eight-story First Bank & Trust Company. Constructed of steel framework with hollow tile and stucco finish, the building also boasted the city's first electric hydraulic elevator for the convenience of visitors. The building consisted of three top stories for hotel space and three middle stories for office space. The bottom two floors provided additional office space and the bank, for which he served as its first president.

Adjacent to the bank building was Lord's Arcade, which fronted both Central Avenue and Main Street. An article in the March 6, 1924 edition of the *Sarasota Times* stated that seven stores in the arcade would face Central Avenue, while nine stores would face Main Street. The article went on to say, "Each store will be finished in individual Spanish design while the main bank building will be an elaborate and clean-cut business structure. The entire building, including stores, will be fireproof."

What once had been one of the most robust real estate markets in the nation struggled when the Florida Land Boom of the mid-1920s soured, followed by the Great Depression in 1929. As a result, Lord had to sell off much of his land holdings at a fraction of their value. The state's comptroller closed the First Bank and Trust Company in 1929; the Palmer Bank eventually took it over. Lord's Arcade was the last property held by the Lord estate. The Palmer Bank also purchased and managed it until the bank's sale in 1972. Both the bank building and the arcade were demolished in 1999.

The Lords left Sarasota in 1930 and relocated to Chicago. Franc died there on April 9, 1936, followed by her husband of fifty years some eight months later. In ill health for some time, Lord died at the age of seventy-six on Christmas Eve. He is buried, along with Franc and other family members, in the Lord family plot at Bradenton's Manasota Cemetery.

He was a man tall in stature and large of frame, and it is said that Joseph Haley Lord's enthusiasm could be very convincing in touting the many benefits of living along Florida's Suncoast. Because of his confidence in the area's future, many invested in the region. Perhaps none believed in his vision more so than Bertha Honoré Palmer. They would eventually become partners in transforming that vision into reality.

THE BUSINESSWOMAN

January 23, 1910—a cold and blustery Sunday in Chicago as Bertha Honoré Palmer sat in her home, nicknamed "the Castle," reading the *Chicago Tribune*. As the winter wind howled off Lake Michigan, an advertisement caught her eye, enticing readers to consider purchasing tracts of land, suitable for growing citrus, along beautiful Sarasota Bay in sunny Florida. Readers were encouraged to contact J.H. Lord of the real estate office of Lord & Edwards, in the city's Marquette Building.

Mrs. Palmer asked her father, Henry (H.H.) Honoré, who maintained an office in the same building, to seek out this Lord fellow and learn more about this investment opportunity. That request would be the spark that would change not only the life of the woman known as the Queen of Chicago but also the landscape of the Suncoast.

At sixty-one years of age, Bertha Palmer was the personification of modern womanhood at the turn of the twentieth century. The widow of Chicago real estate tycoon Potter Palmer, she included presidents, kings and other notable figures of the time among her close friends. With stately homes also in London; Paris; Bar Harbor, Maine; and the Isle of Wight, the world was her stage. The French artist Auguste Rodin sculpted her likeness. And with a fortune of $8 million left to her by her late husband, she was the consummate businesswoman. Little wonder she was chosen chairman of the board of Lady Managers for the World's Columbian Exposition in Chicago in 1893.

At her father's urging, Joseph Lord visited Palmer at her palatial mansion on North Lake Shore Drive. He convinced the wealthy socialite of the vast opportunities that existed along Florida's Gulf Coast. When Palmer decided that the opportunity was worthy of further investigation, Lord sent a telegram to Arthur B. Edwards, his business partner in Sarasota: "Mrs. Potter Palmer coming to Sarasota. Wonderful chance to give Sarasota worldwide advertising. Prepare place for her and party of four. You know what to tell her. She will buy heavily if interested."

Portrait of Bertha Palmer. *Venice Historical Resources.*

Born and raised in the Venice area, A.B. Edwards was orphaned at the age of fifteen and cared for three of his younger brothers. He was elected the town's first tax assessor in 1907 and was a big promoter of growth in Sarasota. In addition to his real estate partnership with Lord, Edwards also served as an agent for acquiring the rights-of-way for the Seaboard Airline Railway (SAL), which eventually extended its line from Sarasota to Venice. He also eventually served as the first mayor of Sarasota when it was incorporated as a city on December 6, 1913.

Although he had received little formal schooling, Edwards probably knew more about Sarasota than anyone. In preparing for Mrs. Palmer's arrival, he set about tidying up the rustic town of 963 residents. First, he had to secure a place for the Palmer entourage to stay. The Belle Haven Inn, which was the only hotel in town, was in such a state of disrepair that Edwards knew it would not be suitable for a woman of her wealth and position. Instead, he convinced a local physician, Dr. Jack Halton, to temporarily relocate his medical practice and take over the sanitarium he operated, which offered a commanding view of Sarasota Bay. With a good deal of renovation and borrowed furniture, they were able to transform the sanitarium into a makeshift hotel they renamed the Halton House.

Palmer arrived in Sarasota on February 10 aboard her private railroad car. She was accompanied by her father; her brother, Adrian; and her two sons, Honoré and Potter Jr. Upon arrival, the celebrated socialite described the frontier community as "refreshingly quaint." She would spend much of her time in the company of Edwards, touring the lands she would eventually purchase.

On a cruise with Edwards into Little Sarasota Bay, Palmer was enamored of the natural beauty of the land. Upon deciding that property in Osprey would be the site of her personal estate, she purchased 13 acres of land for $11,000. Palmer eventually expanded the property to nearly 350 acres and enlarged the existing residence, which she renamed The Oaks. By 1911, she was well on her way to transforming the estate into a tropical paradise that she considered as beautiful as her favorite place, the Bay of Naples.

In that spring of 1910, Palmer had the wealth and connections to spend the rest of her life socializing with the world's elite while enjoying all the luxuries her station in life afforded. Instead, she chose to follow in her father, brother and late husband's footsteps by purchasing and developing this untamed land. In the end, she would own 218 square miles, or 140,000 acres of land, which included some 25 miles of shoreline property. By the time Sarasota County was created in 1921, the Palmer family owned as much as one-third of the new county.

By June, to manage her properties, Palmer had created the Sarasota-Venice Company, with Adrian serving as president and Lord as vice-president. Her two sons, both of whom had graduated from Harvard, held the positions of secretary and treasurer.

The company established two agricultural communities in Sarasota: the Bee Ridge Farms and the Osprey Farms. Palmer also purchased fifteen thousand acres of land around the headwaters of the Myakka River for a ranch, which she called Meadowsweet Pastures.

Palmer considered the land around today's Venice, with its many bays and ready access to the Gulf of Mexico, as the perfect environment where the well-to-do could relax and recreate in an idyllic setting. There needed to be better transportation to get there, however, for that vision to be realized. Roads to the area were almost nonexistent. She pressured the railroad to extend a spur from her Fruitville Farms station south.

The Oaks. *Sarasota County History Center.*

Even though only about twenty-five families were living in the Venice area at the time, the railroad soon began laying track, with service beginning the following year. The February 23, 1911 edition of the *Sarasota Times* stated, "The Seaboard Airline Railroad has surveyed and graded an extension of its line through this property southwest to the town of Venice, four miles of rail have been laid to the first station south of Fruitville, named Palmer, in honor of Mrs. Palmer."

While her efforts were successful in getting the railroad to provide access to her property, the result was not without its controversy. The area encompassing Venice was originally referred to as Horse and Chaise, based on a tree line viewed from the Gulf Coast. When Darwin Curry made application in May 1888 to establish a post office in the area, that name was too long to be approved by the U.S. Post Office. He proposed the name then be Venice, on the suggestion of his brother-in-law, Levi Knight. The new name seemed to be a good fit, as the abundance of bays in the area reminded folks of its cultured Italian counterpart. Serving a population of just sixty people, Curry would serve as the area's first postmaster and would travel by horse to the Osprey Post Office to pick up the local mail.

Palmer took a liking to the name Venice and wanted to use it to identify her property a mile south. At her urging, the railway had extended its line to a point located near the present-day corner of Nokomis and Tampa Avenues, with a freight car serving as the ticket office. It seemed only fitting, she said, that the train "depot" should carry the Venice name.

In January 1912, the railroad elected to name the southernmost depot Venice. About the same time, the U.S. Postal Service announced that it would be relocating its office to the site about a mile southeast as well. The residents of the original Venice were reluctant to give it up, however, and put up a fight. What ensued was a lot of confusion, a flurry of letters and name-calling on both sides of the issue. Unfortunately, Jesse Knight, one of the area's original settlers, had never bothered to plat the settlement or define its boundaries.

The controversy concluded in 1915 when the postal service elected to move the Venice Post Office to its new location near the train depot that shared its name and into the building Palmer had constructed for just that purpose.

Having lost the battle, the residents of the old Venice were not about to formally adopt the name of Potter, the name of Bertha's late husband. They eventually settled on a name submitted by a W.L. Dunn: Nokomis. The Dunn family had migrated to the area from Minnesota, the home of the

Original train station in Venice built for Bertha Palmer. *Venice Historical Resources.*

mythical Hiawatha, made famous by poet Henry Wadsworth Longfellow. In his poem, Nokomis was the name of Hiawatha's grandmother.

With the naming controversy behind her, Palmer once again focused on developing Venice as an ideal playground for the wealthy—a place where the sun-bound visitors could swim, fish, hunt and enjoy the many activities available along Florida's Gulf Coast.

The Sarasota-Venice Company enlisted W.M. Tuttle in February 1915 to survey and file a plat for a small community in Venice. The plat consisted of four square blocks along the Seaboard Airline Railroad (SAL) tracks, intersected by six streets. Present-day Nokomis Street would have been the easternmost intersecting street. She also approached New York City architect Charles Wellford Leavitt for help in designing an "attractive resort and sporting center" where winter visitors with means could recreate in this proposed paradise.

Palmer envisioned a luxurious resort, comparable to anything Henry Flagler had built on Florida's east coast, that would take advantage of spectacular views of the Gulf as well as Venice Bay. By October of that year, Leavitt had submitted his proposed plans, which Palmer and associates immediately rejected as too costly. Instead of developing her idea for an elaborate resort adjacent to the Gulf, the architect envisioned creating an entire city, complete with schools, a commercial district, churches and residences stretching from Venice Bay to Lemon Bay.

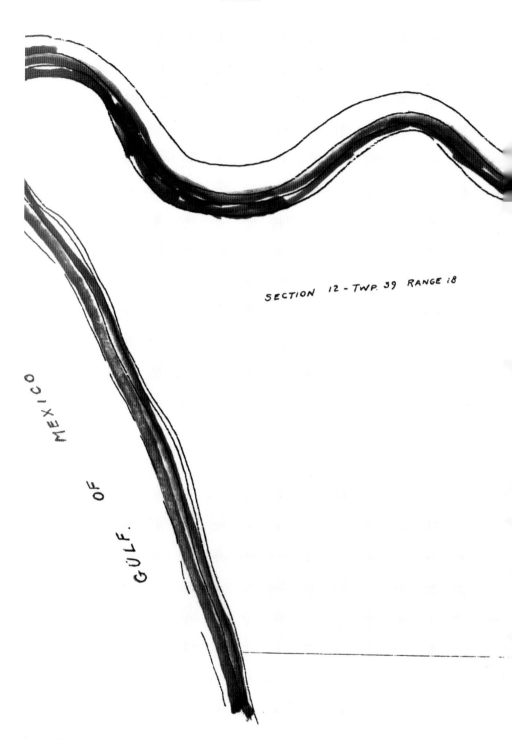

SECTION 12 - TWP. 39 RANGE 18

GULF. OF MEXICO

A 1915 Venice plat. *Venice Historical Resources.*

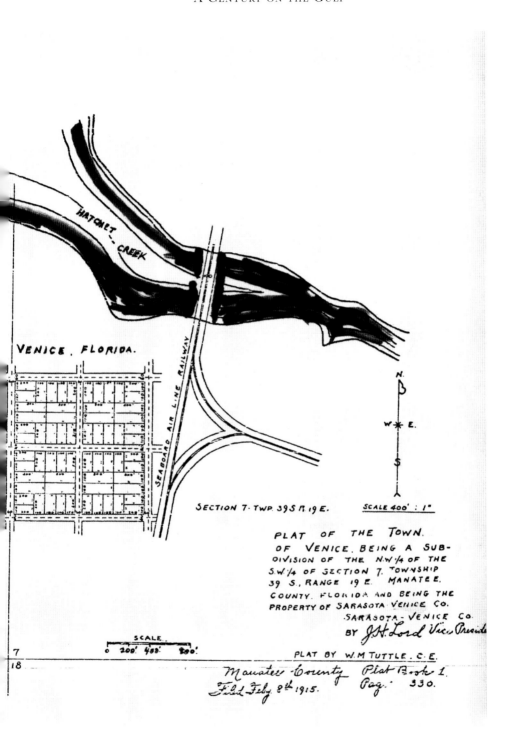

HATCHET CREEK

VENICE, FLORIDA.

SEABOARD AIR LINE RAILWAY

N.
W — E.
S.

SECTION 7. TWP. 39 S. R. 19 E.

SCALE 400' : 1"

PLAT OF THE TOWN.
OF VENICE. BEING A SUB-
DIVISION OF THE N.W.¼ OF THE
S.W.¼ OF SECTION 7. TOWNSHIP
39 S. RANGE 19 E. MANATEE.
COUNTY. FLORIDA AND BEING THE
PROPERTY OF SARASOTA-VENICE CO.
SARASOTA-VENICE CO.
BY J.H. Lord Vice President

SCALE.
0   200' 400' 800'

PLAT BY W.M TUTTLE. C.E.

Manatee County   Plat Book 1.
Filed Feby 8th 1915.   Pag. 330.

7
18

27

To complete his plan, she said in a letter, would force the company to demand an unrealistic asking price of $3,700 for improved lands, while current prices were going for $600 to $1,000 per acre. She reminded Leavitt that the company's purpose was "to enable us to sell it at a profit." Bertha Palmer was a woman who enjoyed beauty in many forms, but like the men in her life, she was foremost about making a profit.

With Leavitt's design for the city of Venice shelved, Palmer turned her attention to another idea for drawing wealthy visitors to the area. Even though the world was at war, the Sarasota-Venice Company began developing a twenty-five-acre close-to-nature rustic resort in Venice to be called Eagle Point Camp.

Located on a piece of land that jutted into Venice Bay, between Hatchet and Curry Creeks, the respite for winter visitors was modeled on another resort she was familiar with called the Teepee. Located in the foothills of the Rocky Mountains near Sheridan, Wyoming, the Teepee was owned and operated by a charismatic Englishman named M.T.L. "Mike" Evans, who offered his well-to-do visitors a relaxing place to fish, hunt, ride horses and get away from city life in a temperate summer climate. Thanks in large part to his charming personality, Evans soon had a following of visitors from major cities throughout the nation who returned each season.

Palmer lured Evans to Florida's Gulf Coast with the intent of having him build and manage Eagle Point Camp. The plan was that Evans would manage the Teepee during the summer months and Eagle Point Camp during the winter season.

Construction began in the summer of 1916. The Sarasota-Venice Company, which owned the property and leased it to Evans, dredged and dug a channel for a boat basin. It also built a two-story clubhouse containing a downstairs dining room where all guests ate together, with bachelor's quarters located upstairs. Ten guest cottages with wrap-around porches made of native pine and painted barn red with white trim also encompassed the camp. Near the dwellings was a tennis court.

Calling it the "most up-to-date and modern equipped resort on the west coast," the *Sarasota Times* described it as "a winter camp, where all the pleasures of sport on water and land can be enjoyed by the guests. The location is superb and the plans of the proprietor will make it a popular resort for northern people."

Evans welcomed the first guests, many of whom had followed him from Teepee, to Eagle Point Camp on January 11, 1917. Days were spent sunning on Eagle Point Beach, an area maintained on Treasure Island (today's Casey Key), or catching tarpon and other sporting fish in Venice Bay or the Gulf. The camp also maintained a hunting preserve to the south where guests rode horses with their prepared lunches tied to their saddles. And of course, Bertha Palmer made sure there was plenty of opportunity to tour the area by car and boat with the goal of selling them property in this newfound paradise.

News of Eagle Point Camp grew quickly, and Evans purchased the resort from the Sarasota-Venice Company in 1918. It was during that summer that the first paved road between Sarasota and Venice passed through the complex.

F. Kingsbury Curtis and his wife, Cornelia, were early visitors to Eagle Point. A patent attorney in New York City, he invested in real estate as a hobby. He and his wife purchased the resort from Evans in 1923. Hosting winter guests until 1988, the property later became a gated community.

One of the last projects Bertha pursued before her death in 1918 was the creation of a golf and country club in Venice. It was to be the realization of a "sporting club" she had envisioned as part of the resort she had hoped Leavitt would design. Lamar Rankin had worked for the Sarasota-Venice Company, selling parcels in the Bee Ridge Farms Project and elsewhere. In a letter to Palmer in late 1917, he proposed the building of a 250-acre waterfront country club "that would be easy for you to market, at very little

F. Kingsbury Curtis, wife Cornelia McClanahan Curtis and her parents, Helen and George McClanahan, taken at Eagle Point. *Venice Historical Resources.*

outlay." He estimated a profit of as much as $75,000 could be realized from such a project. By the end of the year, Rankin was in Chicago, selling $2,500 memberships to the club. Some memberships were sold, but the war and difficulty in reaching the area by train stalled the project. Creating a golf club in Venice would have to wait.

In 1917, Bertha Palmer was diagnosed with breast cancer and underwent a mastectomy in New York City. Unfortunately, the cancer metastasized. She kept her condition private while continuing her various projects. Palmer died at The Oaks, her beloved home in Osprey, on May 5, 1918, one day after the sixteenth anniversary of Potter's death. She was sixty-nine years old. The cause of her death was listed as pneumonia, and family members reported that she only took ill about a week before her death. In announcing her death, the *Sarasota Herald-Tribune* said, "There can be no grief at the end of such a journey."

THE PALMER FAMILY, PRIMARILY led by her two sons and brother, continued to invest in various projects throughout the Suncoast. The Palmer National Bank and Trust Company formally opened on March 20, 1929, a mere seven months before the stock market crash and beginning of the Great Depression. The first depositor in the newly formed bank was the family's old friend Joseph Lord. The bank would go on to purchase and occupy the building Lord built to house his own banking venture.

Chicago never lost its bond with the Palmers. Bertha is buried in that city, next to her husband, with many family members interred nearby.

"WHERE THE TAMIAMI TRAIL MEETS THE OPEN GULF OF MEXICO"

Along with visionaries Joseph Lord and Bertha Palmer, others living along the Gulf Coast realized the potential for developing Florida's forgotten frontier. One of the biggest stumbling blocks, however, was the difficulty in navigating this untamed wilderness.

By the early twentieth century, Henry Flagler had built his railroad down Florida's east coast, connecting all the cities from Jacksonville to Key West. Henry Plant, on the other hand, built his railroad through Georgia, extending his tracks across Florida and ending in Tampa. That left much of the land to the south largely unnavigable except by water or horse. Roads consisted of little more than sandy ruts through the scrub—or, as some were called, "wish to God roads," as in "I wish to God I had not taken this road." Carrying a shovel to dig their Model Ts out of the sand almost became a necessity.

Sarasota County remained the southern half of Manatee County until May 14, 1921. Part of the growing resentment that led to the split was due to the lack of adequate roads. County government seemed more intent on connecting Bradenton to other cities in Florida than building roads to the south.

Prominent men, led by Sarasota Mayor A.B. Edwards, formed a "Sarasota Good Roads Booster" committee to promote the need for better roads. In 1911, the county approved a $250,000 bond to construct a road from the Hillsborough County line to Sarasota. Three years later, residents created the Sarasota-Venice Road and Bridge District to extend the highway to

Venice. About the same time, some good road boosters in Englewood were making plans to build a road north to Venice.

An editorial in the *Sarasota Times* noted, "If we wait until we can afford to issue bonds for roads and bridges, we will never get them." Voters approved a bond issue to pay for the Sarasota to Venice connection on March 16, 1915, with seven Venice residents voting in favor and one opposed.

Plans initially called for a fifteen-foot-wide road. But before officials sold the bonds, they realized that the $250,000 would only cover the cost of a nine-foot-wide road. Realizing that a nine-foot road was better than nothing, they again approved the issue on January 16, 1916.

Continental Public Works Company of New York won the contract to construct the asphalt road, complete with concrete berm, for $280,663. Contracts were also let for bridges on the Venice-bound road, as well as one from the mainland to Siesta Key.

Work on the roads progressed at a rapid pace. The September 20, 1917 edition of the *Sarasota Times* announced that the road from Tampa to Sarasota was mostly complete and that it was now possible to travel between the two cities in just three and a half hours.

By the summer of 1918, the stretch of road connecting Sarasota and Venice, dubbed by some as the "Velvet Highway," was essentially complete. At its southern end, the road snaked through the winter resort of Eagle Point Camp, offering motorists a splendid view of Venice Bay.

The road then crossed a wooden bridge to the southern shore of the bay and through what eventually would become the city of Venice. After World War I, it was extended south to Englewood. There it terminated, and anyone who ventured farther south did so at his or her own risk. It was not until 1947 that the two-lane road between Sarasota and Venice was widened from eighteen to twenty-four feet and resurfaced at a cost of $380,000.

As roads throughout the Suncoast continued to proliferate, there was a growing interest in forming a highway system extending to the end of the Florida peninsula.

In April 1915, Frances W. Perry, president of the Fort Myers Chamber of Commerce, and Miami developer James F. Jaudon met in Tallahassee with state officials to discuss the idea of constructing what they called at the time a "Miami to Marco Highway" that would connect the two coastal cities. There was another meeting in Orlando just two months later that resulted in the formation of the Central Florida Highway Association. At that meeting, Perry made a resolution, which E.P. Dickie of Tampa seconded, to extend the highway from Tampa to Marco and then due east to Miami. Work on

The nine-foot road from Sarasota to Venice just north of Eagle Point Camp, circa 1916.
Venice Historical Resources.

the "Tamiami Trial" began on August 3, 1915, when the Dade County Board of Commissioners provided the services of their engineer to survey the first 3.5 miles of the highway from Miami.

Also in 1915, the state legislature created the Florida State Road Department. The following year, Congress approved the Bankhead Act, which provided federal aid for improving highways. Florida increased the Road Department's authority the following year with the intention of joining West Coast cities with hard-surfaced roads. The department worked with each county or district, which was responsible for funding their portion of the trail.

It looked like smooth sailing for the new highway that would transform Florida's peninsula. Fate intervened, however, in the form of a world war, a devastating hurricane, the creation of three new counties along the route and a Florida land bust that would stagnate the economy.

Florida's Road Department ran out of funds in 1922 to complete the last segment of the highway through the Everglades, and the project seemed doomed. Naples businessman Barron Collier, however, came to the rescue.

Construction of the Sarasota-Venice segment of the Tamiami Trail. *Venice Historical Resources.*

He pledged to fund completion of the highway if the Florida legislature would agree to establish a new county and name it after him. The following year, the state created Collier County from the southern half of Lee County, and finishing the Tamiami Trail was back on track.

Easier said than done. Building a hard-surface highway through Florida's "River of Grass" proved a formidable challenge. Some of the workers, nicknamed "Tamiami Trailblazers," died in the process. Wading through neck-deep water, workmen used dynamite to blast free the limestone under the muck that was then dredged and used to build the roadbed. Seminole Indian guides led the way, and sharpshooters remained vigilant to keep away the alligators and other predators. Clouds of disease-carrying mosquitos were a constant threat.

The Tamiami Trail officially opened on April 26, 1928. A two-day motorcade of cars carrying dignitaries from Tampa to Miami was planned to celebrate the milestone. Weeks before the opening ceremony, Dr. Fred and Louella Albee drove the route with permission from the state's Road Department. Louella reported a distance of two hundred miles from Miami to Venice. The *Sarasota Herald* described the Tamiami Trail as "undoubtedly the most important highway on the west coast of Florida today."

On April 25, a caravan of nearly two hundred automobiles left Tampa for the celebratory trek to Miami. The night before, the participants from all over the state listened to a speech by Florida Governor John Martin on the impact the highway would have on the western part of the state. Upon arriving in Sarasota, the caravan picked up another one hundred cars, including businessman Joseph H. Lord. The motorcade eventually reached Venice, where Mayor Ned Worthington cut the ceremonial ribbon marking the event. It would be one of the last events Worthington would officiate before leaving town when the Brotherhood of Locomotive Engineers pulled out of the Venice project. With similar events being held in each town along the route, some five hundred automobiles were expected to complete the caravan before it reached Miami.

Local businessmen and civic leaders were so excited by the potential the new road could bring to the Suncoast that they began using the following slogan in their advertising: "Venice Where the Tamiami Trail Meets the Gulf of Mexico." When the *Venice Gondolier* newspaper began publishing in March 1946, it included the slogan in its masthead. The Tamiami Trail,

Automobiles traveling the Tamiami Trail, 1927. *Florida Memory.*

celebrated in both song and story as the "Road of Enchantment," completed what reporters of the day called "Florida's last frontier."

The trail would eventually be replaced by Interstate 75 in the early 1980s, and many of the roadside businesses and attractions that had prospered for decades would gradually disappear. In all, the Tamiami Trail took years to build, cost $8 million and required 2.6 million sticks of dynamite to construct. The 264-mile highway officially exists from State Road 60 in Tampa to U.S. 1 in Miami. The north–south leg is officially known as U.S. Highway 41, and the east–west segment is designated State Road 90.

THE DOCTOR AND HIS WIFE

Dr. Fred Albee and his wife, Louella, had already become world travelers by the time they first stepped off the train in Sarasota, Florida, in late February 1917. The forty-year-old orthopedic surgeon, however, would quickly fall under the charms of the Suncoast. "Its climate, its sunshine, its pleasant way of life, its fishing, all of these things have been an unending delight to one who originally discovered the secrets of nature the hard way, on a Maine farm," he wrote in his autobiography, *A Surgeon's Fight to Rebuild Men*.

The Albees had come to Florida's Gulf Coast at the urging of Louella's cousin and her husband, who wintered at Sarasota's "Maine Colony," located near Philippi Creek. "We arrived at night and went directly to the Maine Colony," Louella later recounted in her own memoir, *Doctor and I*. "The next morning, bright and early, Doctor was up and about—and he too was sold on Florida before he had even seen much of it. Our stay there lasted only eight days—yet, before we left, he had purchased the entire village of Nokomis." At a price of $100 per acre, Albee purchased 112 acres of land in Nokomis that bordered on Roberts and Dona Bay. He would go on to own some thirty miles of waterfront land in the area, totaling some 2,500 acres, including that which would become the city of Venice.

Fred Albee was born on April 13, 1876, in Alna, Maine. The oldest of seven children, he said he was able to carry his "share of the load" on the family's hardscrabble, one-hundred-acre farm by the age of eight. Even as a child, Fred dreamed of one day becoming a surgeon. He fashioned a "medical case" out of an old salt box, and his mother gave him bits of dough to make bread pills. In addition to Albee's interest in medicine, all things mechanical and how they worked also fascinated him. Whenever anything in the house or on the farm was broken, he said, the family would take the item to him for repair.

One of his childhood experiences would set the course for the rest of his life. Albee often accompanied his maternal grandfather, Charles Houdlette, when the former carpenter and "tree grafter" would graft apple trees for farmers. "I went about the countryside with him," he wrote, "carrying bundles of apple scions which I handed up to him to graft." He would later marvel at the sweet apples growing on sour-apple trees. That time spent in the apple orchards, he would say, "focused my interest on the mechanics of the human body with special relation to the levers, hinges, ball and socket joints, that make up the body structure."

Albee graduated from Bowdoin College in 1899 and from Harvard Medical School in 1903. It was at Harvard that he began to think about how to apply what he had learned from his grandfather to the human body. He performed his first bone graft operation in New York City just three years out of Harvard, and the procedure drew a great deal of attention from the medical field. "The mechanic, the tree grafter, and the surgeon in me," he would say, "went into consultation."

Albee met his future wife, Louella May Berry, in New York City, where she worked in the millinery business. They married in 1907, and she would go on to serve as his able partner as the young surgeon's medical practice continued to grow and gain worldwide attention.

In 1917, America entered World War I, shortly after the Albees had purchased land in Nokomis. By this time, Albee had performed hundreds of bone graft surgeries and had invented the high-speed Albee bone mill (1909) and the Albee orthopedic table (1915), which enabled him to conduct the delicate procedure in as little as nine minutes. He never bothered to have either of his inventions patented because he was more interested in enriching the lives of people worldwide. "He felt that he was not only teaching his methods, but helping the more unfortunate human beings," Louella Albee wrote.

Louella gave birth to a son, Fred Albee Jr., whom the couple called Ted, on February 3, 1918. Ted would himself become an orthopedic surgeon and, also following service as an officer in the Army Medical Corps, began private practice in Daytona Beach in 1954. He practiced medicine on Florida's east coast until his death on December 2, 1994.

Colonel Fred H. Albee in World War I uniform, no date. *Venice Historical Resources.*

As a major in the Army's Medical Reserve Corps, Albee convinced the government to build a rehabilitative hospital for injured soldiers near their home in Colonia, New Jersey. Congress appropriated $3.5 million to build General Hospital No. 3, providing two thousand beds and a total of 110 buildings spread over two hundred acres. More than six thousand soldiers were treated before the hospital was closed in 1919, and Albee performed at least half of all the bone graft surgeries on soldiers during the war.

Meanwhile, the couple was becoming more familiar with their new Florida property. "How well I recall our first visit to Nokomis!" Louella Albee wrote. "We found nothing there but palmetto land, cabbage palms and beautiful palm trees, and the remnants of an old stockade." The Albees built a hotel in 1922 on the site of that former stockade. They called it the Pollyanna Inn. The hotel was located adjacent to Dona Bay on a new road that would later become known as the Tamiami Trail. In 1925, on property across Pocono Trail, Fred established the Venice-Nokomis Bank and formed the Venice-Nokomis Chamber of Commerce. It is no wonder that the entrepreneurial surgeon would eventually be called the "Father of Nokomis."

The Albees moved into their new Mediterranean-style house on February 14, 1923, which they would name Point o' Palms. The house, built at a cost of about $50,000, sat on five acres of land, facing Dona Bay. Louella Albee stated that the property enjoyed an abundance of grapefruit trees but lacked orange trees. No problem for Fred Albee, however, as he simply grafted orange scions onto the grapefruit trees, thereby offering an ample supply of both fruits.

In August 1924, Albee purchased from the Sarasota-Venice Company the 1,468-acre parcel for $185,000 that would eventually become the city of Venice. With the intent of fulfilling Bertha Palmer's original vision to build a city on the land, he enlisted the services of John Nolen, an international leader in urban planning. "I think you have a very good idea of the geography of this spot," he wrote in a letter to Nolen on August 5, 1924. "It is really a modern Venice. There are so many bays, riverlets, etc. It ought to make a

Polyanna Inn, 1922. *Venice Historical Resources.*

most attractive town and what do you think I should do in the beginning?" Nolen produced elaborately colored maps of his plans for developing the city, with suggested locations for hotels, parks, theaters and businesses.

Homes began to spring up throughout the burgeoning community. Albee hired the Roger C. Rice Company to market the property, including a brochure titled *Venice-Nokomis: The White City on the Gulf*, the color referring to the white stucco exteriors of the buildings.

He also built at 811 Esplanade a three-story Venice Bath House & Beach Casino, which also included a pier. Built in 1925, the bathhouse was largely destroyed in a 1926 hurricane and would be rebuilt in the mid-1930s several hundred yards to the south.

At the time, the Florida bubble of prosperity was about as "distended as it could possibly be," Albee wrote in his memoir. "But my surgical practice had expanded, and when I had that section of Venice, now called Nokomis, satisfactorily started on its path of development, I found that much of my city-creation urge had been satisfied. When my wife pointed out that the building of a complete city, on top of my professional work would be too much of a strain for me, and urged me to sell my blue-printed city, I listened to her counsel, and recognizing its wisdom, let it be known that Venice could be bought." Without advertising the property for sale, Fred soon found himself with ten potential buyers. The one seemingly most qualified was the Brotherhood of Locomotive Engineers (BLE), the Cleveland-based union

Point o' Palms, circa 1921. *Venice Historical Resources.*

representing some ninety-one thousand railroad workers. The BLE enjoyed controlling interest in some thirty-five banks across the nation, as well as an elaborate underwriting service for stocks and bonds. It seemed to have the available assets to build an entire city from scratch.

To cover some previous bad investments, BLE executives began looking for speculative opportunities in Florida that promised to help quickly recover their losses. Venice soon surfaced by the summer of 1925 as just such an opportunity. They purchased several parcels, including Albee's 1,468 acres, at a cost of $1,012,877. The BLE's total holdings amounted to more than 30,000 acres, extending from the Gulf of Mexico all the way eastward to the Myakka River.

In a letter dated July 29, 1925, Albee informed Nolen that he had sold the Venice property to the BLE, but that he had encouraged the union to retain his services to design the city. "I have recommended to them that they put in a canal according to Government survey, which would complete the inland water ways between Tampa and Miami," he added. "This canal would run from the Bay of Venice to the Miakka [*sic*] River. It would serve not only as a medium of navigation, and the missing link to inland waterways on the

West Coast of Florida, but also the main drainage canal to that great area of land." With the future development of Venice now in the hands of the BLE, Albee was able to refocus his pursuits on further development of Nokomis and the Bay Point subdivision. He also could spend more time enjoying his favorite pastime of fishing the waters along the Suncoast.

In addition to sharing time between their homes in Nokomis and Colonia, New Jersey, allowing Albee to attend to his growing medical practice, the couple traveled throughout Europe and South America, giving lectures to other doctors on how to conduct his bone-grafting procedure. Louella Albee said they crossed the Atlantic together some thirty-eight times during their travels.

Toward the end of the decade, the Florida bubble burst, and the BLE was forced to abandon its Venice project. "As holder of a large percentage of the mortgages in Venice, I had much of the property back in my hands," wrote Albee. "What to do with it was my next problem."

Ever since the Albees had been coming to Florida, Fred thought the area was the ideal place to start a health center. "To set up a hospital where the

Aerial view of Nokomis looking east in the 1940s. The Polyanna Inn is in the center, with the Venice-Nokomis Bank to the right. Dr. Albee's Point o' Palms is in lower right. *Venice Historical Resources.*

Florida Medical Center, circa 1930. *Venice Historical Resources.*

tubercular conditions of bones and joints which I was operating on in less favorable climates would have the best possible assistance from nature." In 1933, in the midst of the Great Depression, Fred purchased the empty Park View Hotel and established his Florida Medical Center. He also approached the Seaboard Airline Railroad to consider extending its express "Orange Blossom Special" service from New York City to Venice. This made it possible for his patients to recover more quickly in Venice's ideal weather. The Center soon converted into a volunteer hospital, offering all types of services as well as making it a post-graduate medical teaching institution. Conferences were held at the facility, drawing medical professionals from all over the world.

Albee increasingly believed that "vitamins play an enormous part in human health and in disease prevention." For that reason, he created Albee Farms, consisting of 6,400 acres of nearby land, to provide the center with fruits and vegetables grown under special conditions, offering the maximum benefits of minerals and vitamins. A dairy also was established where free-range cows grazed on mineralized grass and soaked up the Florida sunshine.

Albee loved flowers. In addition to growing fruits and vegetables on their farm, the Albees also grew gladiolus. They traveled to Holland to study the bulb culture there and purchased 1 million bulbs. The flowers were shipped to many northern cities, with New York City being their largest market.

During the height of the season, the farm was shipping as many as 2,500 dozen gladiolus spikes per day. They also canned and shipped grapefruit juice as well as small potatoes. Albee's younger brother, Stephen, moved his family to Venice so that he could oversee the Albee Farms operation, as well as assist with some of Albee's other entrepreneurial pursuits. The two brothers were close, and having Steve in Venice to oversee Fred's many projects provided the couple peace of mind.

The Medical Center proved successful and continued operation until 1942, when the Army Air Corps established a pilot training base in Venice and took over the facility to serve as its army hospital.

One of the biggest challenges the surgeon faced was the amount of time spent traveling by train back and forth between Venice and his medical practice in New York City. Louella Albee once remarked that the railroad's acronym, SAL, actually stood for "she's always late." Albee solved the problem in the late 1930s when he became a pilot and purchased a five-passenger Stinson airplane he nicknamed "Reliance." This significantly reduced his travel time to his practice and also enabled his nephew, Steve Albee Jr., to ferry his patients from all over the Americas to the Medical Center. "Doctor was much like a small boy with this plane—the way he enjoyed it no end," wrote Louella Albee. In 1935, work began to construct a grass-strip runway to serve the Venice community on land donated by Albee. The runway began just south of Venice Avenue and ended near what

Dr. Fred Albee and his pilot, nephew Stephen Albee Jr., with Dr. Albee's ambulance "Reliance," circa 1940. *Venice Historical Resources.*

Louella May Berry Albee, circa 1930. *Venice Historical Resources.*

was then the city's municipal golf course. The runway was formally dedicated on January 23, 1939, and sparked a good deal of interest among many Venice residents in learning to fly.

The Albees continued to generously support their newfound home over the years. Since the BLE had not made plans for any local churches, they donated land on which to build the Venice-Nokomis Methodist Church, St. Marks Episcopal Church and the Epiphany Cathedral. And at the end of 1941, he donated to Venice the 570-foot stretch of beach fronting the city's beach casino.

While Fred was engaged in his various development projects, Louella also found many ways to serve the community. She was the founder and first president of the Venice-Nokomis Woman's Club and would serve in that capacity two more times during the next fifteen years. She donated the funds that paid for the local library, which was named after her. Louella also organized the first Girl Scout Troop and Camp Fire Girls in Venice.

Fred Albee died on February 14, 1945, and his holdings in the Venice-Nokomis area were sold to a St. Petersburg group headed by Robert S. Baynard. Louella died at Sarasota Hospital on February 4, 1956, at the age of eighty. "How my husband loved every inch of the land around Venice and Nokomis!" Louella wrote. "He was like a little child whenever we went South. I often asked him why he enjoyed it all so much. The professional and other responsibilities there certainly entailed many trying problems. His only reply would be, 'I love it!'"

THE BROTHERHOOD

By the mid-1920s, the Florida Land Boom was at its peak, and orthopedic surgeon Dr. Fred Albee was busy investing in his Nokomis projects while also making plans for development of his ideal city he called Venice Beach. With an expanding medical practice, however, and at the urging of his wife, he realized that building an entire city from scratch might be too much of a strain.

Albee soon identified ten potential buyers for his 1,468 acres of land, but one suitor clearly stood out from the rest: the Brotherhood of Locomotive Engineers (BLE). Initially formed on May 8, 1863, as the Brotherhood of the Footboard, the BLE was the first labor union in America to provide its members with insurance (conventional insurance providers considered railroad work too dangerous). By 1925, the BLE boasted some ninety-one thousand members and had accumulated more than $150 million in assets. It enjoyed controlling interest in some thirty-five banks nationwide and maintained underwriting capability. From Albee's perspective, the BLE certainly had the deep pockets to build Venice.

The union sent a committee to Florida in August 1925 to search for investment opportunities throughout the state. The purpose was to generate enough income to cover some financial losses that had amounted to several million dollars. The committee considered several properties in the state, including land near Fort Myers, but in the end concluded that the Venice property could likely generate the most profit.

The BLE Realty Company was formed on September 4, 1925, to oversee management of the Venice project. George T. Webb, who served as vice-president of the BLE's Investment Company, was named executive vice-president of the new venture. Although the initial thought was to flip the land for a modest profit, Webb convinced union officials that much more money could be made by carrying through with Albee's vision for developing the city.

Albee, who had purchased the Palmer property for $185,000 in August 1924, sold it eleven months later to BLE Realty for $1,012,877. The new owners also purchased surrounding property, extending as far east as the Myakka River, in total possessing more than thirty thousand acres of land, purchased at a cost of about $4 million.

The Brotherhood's plans for the area were publicly announced in September 1925. Stating its commitment to the project, BLE Realty was prepared to spend $40 million or "a million a month" to see its vision transformed into reality.

The Sarasota-based Southern Construction Engineers Company was hired to handle surveying the land, particularly that which existed east of the railroad tracks to the Myakka River. To do that, the company was encouraged to at least triple its engineering staff to fast-track the project. Southern Construction declined to expand, however, so the Brotherhood engaged the Washington, D.C.–based consulting firm of Black, McKinney and Stewart to take over the task. A team of 125 engineers, under the leadership of George Youngberg Sr., set about to complete the work as quickly as possible. Youngberg would remain involved in Venice's development after the BLE withdrew from the project and would eventually serve as the city's mayor in 1952.

John Nolen's regional plan for Venice, circa 1924–27. *Cornell University Archives.*

The George A. Fuller Company, which had recently built the BLE's twenty-one-story bank and office building in Cleveland, was hired to do the actual construction of Venice. And notable city planner John Nolen, who was initially hired by Fred Albee to plan the city's design, was retained by the BLE to continue the work. The fifty-six-year-old Nolen, a former student of Frederick Law Olmsted Jr. and one of the world's leading proponents of the city-garden concept of urban design, already had numerous projects underway in Florida. But he saw Venice as having the greatest potential for promoting his ideals and his business.

Prentiss French, like Nolen, was a graduate of Harvard's School of Landscape Architecture. He was hired to oversee the landscaping of Venice. Arriving in January 1926, French established a forty-acre nursery and was responsible for not only landscaping the city's many parks and commercial areas but also ensuring that the residences conformed to the urban plan.

The New York City architectural firm of Walker and Gillette was retained to oversee the design of all company and residential buildings. The decision was made to design all structures in the Mediterranean Revival style, which was popular in other cities throughout Florida at the time. The style was characterized by such architectural characteristics as stucco exteriors, sloping

Planting canary date palms at the BLE Nursery, April 19, 1926. *Venice Historical Resources.*

Fuller Construction Company Building in Venice, circa 1927. *Venice Historical Resources.*

tile roofs and colorful awnings. The firm sent Howard Patterson to serve as resident architect for the project to approve the design of all buildings.

H.N. "Bud" Wimmers came to Venice as assistant treasurer for BLE Realty in January 1926. Because the burgeoning city only yet existed on paper, many of the new employees lived in rental properties in Sarasota and were ferried to and from Venice daily by BLE buses.

At its peak in 1926, the Fuller Company hired more than 4,500 workers, about 500 of them African American, to do the work. The company erected barracks for the workers in an area it called "tent city," just south of Hatchet Creek. A mess hall also was built that served meals in shifts. Black workers lived in separate camps near Laurel and a former turpentine operation. To facilitate the construction, many businesses such as the Venice Tile Company sprang up on site to manufacture needed materials.

Nolen's General Plan for Venice envisioned a sustainable community comprising residential, agricultural, and commercial areas. The residences and business district, located between the Gulf of Mexico and the Seaboard Airline Railroad (SAL) track, would appeal to those vacationers and residents seeking warm winter weather. The land east of the tracks, extending to the Myakka River, would serve as farmland for growing crops that could not only feed the local community but also create a profitable export for northern markets.

The railroad came into the center of Nolen's plans for the city, while the main road entered to the west by way of Eagle Point Camp. To facilitate his design for Venice, the BLE approached the railroad and offered to build a modern train depot in exchange for moving its tracks a quarter mile to the east. The plan was approved, and work began on a modern $48,000 depot that featured waiting rooms for both white and Black passengers, a spacious freight storage room and uploading and receiving platforms. The main highway into Venice was then rerouted to follow the path into town formerly taken by the railroad.

Nolen's plan called for the city's infrastructure to be completed before any buildings were constructed. "Fuller's Army" got busy paving roads, laying storm water pipes and installing electric lights. The city's major thoroughfare, Venice Avenue, was laid out with a two-hundred-foot width in the residential district and an eighty-foot parkway down the center. A horse bridle path was laid with Ocala stone down the center of the median, with rows of orange trees planted on each side. Oak and palm trees lined the sidewalks.

They constructed a state-of-the-art water treatment plant, capable of pumping five hundred gallons per minute from four artesian wells. Wimmers said that BLE Realty's plan was to build everything to meet the community's needs for at least a decade. The water tower, for example, was expected to ultimately serve as many as ten thousand residents.

An ice plant was constructed in nearby Nokomis, adjacent to the SAL tracks. Operating nonstop, the Venice Ice Company could produce twenty tons of ice per day. It not only produced enough ice to serve the area, but it also made it possible to keep locally grown produce fresh until reaching northern markets.

A subsidiary of the BLE Realty, called the Venice Company, was created to handle the sale of properties. It hired dozens of salesmen to escort potential buyers around the burgeoning city in special passenger buses. A sightseeing boat, called the *Raven*, was docked at Casey's Pass to provide visitors the opportunity to view Venice by water. And plenty of activities were planned for guests like fishing trips and picnics on the beach near Fred Albee's bathhouse.

To support the sales effort, the company put into place one of the largest promotional campaigns of its kind in the nation. Writers and editors were hired to produce a tabloid newsletter called *This Week in Venice*, which

Venice Train Depot, 1927. *Venice Historical Resources.*

The Venice Ice Company in Nokomis, 1926. *Venice Historical Resources.*

Bea Brown, daughter of BLE photographer Jay E. Brown, atop a manta ray, 1927.

was shared with visitors and distributed to potential markets in major cities. A professional photographer named Jay Brown took hundreds of photographs that showed the progress being made in building Venice, as well as captured how some of the earliest residents were enjoying life in this southern paradise. One of his most iconic photographs was of his barefoot daughter, Bea, standing on the back of a giant manta ray that had been caught in local waters.

The Venice Company produced and distributed slick flyers, touting the many benefits of living in Venice, to prospective buyers worldwide. Sales representatives were promoting the project in eighty-four cities outside Florida, while a dozen other salesmen traveled all over the country, showing movies of the progress in building Venice. More than one hundred road signs touting the city appeared all over Florida. And full-page advertisements were published in national newspapers and magazines. One such ad, titled "One Hundred Things to Do at Venice," proceeded to list all those activities visitors could do to entertain themselves.

Nationally known artists like Julius Delbos created beautiful watercolor images that captured the idyllic romance of living in such a tropical paradise as Venice, and these images appeared in promotional literature and advertising.

There were also publicity stunts designed to garner national attention. For example, a stunt pilot from Lakeland, Florida, named George Haldeman landed his biplane on Nassau Street to deliver fresh strawberries to the Hotel Venice, which opened in June 1926. And then there were natural opportunities that gained national attention like when Venice farmer John Parker discovered the fossilized skeletal remains of a mammoth in September 1926 on his property that captured the attention of the Smithsonian Institution. Northern newspapers, of course, were always receptive to publishing photographs of bathing beauties enjoying the city's white sandy beaches during the winter months. In December 1926, the Venice Chamber of Commerce organized a nationwide radio broadcast of music featuring the city's own Anthony Lopez Orchestra.

Thanks to the abundance of game fish that populated the nearby bays and Gulf, the Venice Tarpon Club was formed, and anglers from everywhere converged on the area for the annual Tarpon Tournament. The

The Anthony Lopez Orchestra, 1926. *Venice Historical Resources.*

first tournament, held in June 1926, drew some two hundred applicants, all vying for cash prizes. A Tarpon Clubhouse was even established at Casey's Pass, and sports reporters from major newspapers covered the events.

City promoters were always after well-known figures in sports, politics, business, and other occupations to visit Venice and provide endorsements. Thomas Edison, who owned a winter home in Fort Myers, visited numerous times and had his picture taken with local dignitaries. He also was quoted endorsing the Venice project. And Florida Governor John W. Martin, who visited many times and supported the city's development, said, "Your [BLE] organization stands as a monument to the people of the nation today of what unity of purpose will accomplish and what a creed and an understanding will do."

One of the biggest promoters of Venice, of course, was the Seaboard Air Line Railroad, which benefited from the many prospective buyers riding into town on its trains. With advertising provided by the brotherhood, advertisements appeared on its trains, in the terminals it served and throughout its promotional literature.

The BLE Realty's vision for Venice was quickly becoming a reality. Only one permanent building existed in Venice by July 1, 1926. At year's end, however, some 185 buildings had been completed or were under construction, valued at more than $3 million. The city's population had grown from a handful to nearly three thousand residents.

By the end of 1926, workers had grubbed and cleared forty-two thousand acres of land, paved more than eighty-five thousand square yards of concrete streets, dug nearly twenty-two miles of drainage ditches, and strung five miles of high-tension wiring, with two miles of streetlights in operation. Even though Florida's land boom had long since gone bust, the future of the City by the Gulf looked very bright.

THE PLANNERS

By the time the BLE Realty began envisioning its plans for the city of Venice, John Nolen was already considered a worldwide leader of the "city-garden" approach to urban design and was engaged in hundreds of planning projects all over the country. Many of those projects were taking place in Florida cities such as Jacksonville, St. Petersburg, Clewiston and Bellaire near Clearwater—so many projects in the state, in fact, that he established a satellite office in Jacksonville that included his son, John Nolen Jr.

Nolen was no stranger to the Suncoast, having been introduced to the area by Dr. Fred Albee, who engaged him in 1924 to help plan many of his development projects in Nokomis. When Albee sold the land that would become Venice to the BLE Realty Company in 1925, he recommended that it retain Nolen's services in order to provide continuity to the project.

Unlike many of his other projects, where he was "re-designing" existing cities, Nolen saw Venice as an opportunity to create from scratch an ideal community where residents could live, work, and play in the same space. "Venice is the first city built to demonstrate what Florida can do to produce a community that is at once a fine resort of great charm and refreshment and a city serving all the every-day needs of a well-conceived, well-designed, and soundly constructed municipality," he stated in the June 3, 1927 edition of *Venice News*. "The result is an inspiration to those who would make this world a better place to live in."

In keeping with his philosophy of immersing communities into their landscape in a coexistent manner, Nolen designed Venice to take advantage

Left: John Nolen, no date. *Venice Historical Resources.*

Below: John Nolen's plan of Venice, 1926. *Venice Historical Resources.*

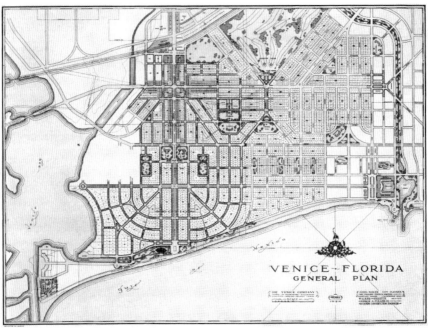

VENICE – FLORIDA
GENERAL PLAN

of the ideal contour of the land bordered by the Gulf of Mexico and its surrounding bays. "We started with an absolutely clean slate, and this gave us an opportunity to change and alter our plans to suit the situation," he said. In choosing an ideal location for a community, he added, "nature led the way and man wisely followed."

He added, "Venice is not only a new city but a city built on new lines. It is thoroughly modern in convenience from the point of view of traffic, practical from the point of view of use, and in a fundamental sense beautiful. Why? Because the site was well chosen."

Born in Philadelphia in 1869 and orphaned as a child, Nolen spent his formative years at Girard College, a local school for orphans. A good student with an interest in urban reform, he graduated with honors from the University of Pennsylvania's Wharton Business School in 1893. Ten years later, he sold his house and used the money to enroll in Harvard University's newly formed graduate School of Landscape Architecture. Just one of eleven students, he studied under noted designers Frederick Law Olmsted Jr. and Arthur Shurtleff. He earned his master's degree from Harvard in 1905 and, while still a student, took on his first commission, overseeing a design project with the City of Charlotte, North Carolina. He opened an office in Cambridge, Massachusetts, upon graduation and within two decades was recognized as a leader in city planning.

Nolen's plan for Venice was fundamentally pedestrian friendly. In keeping with his philosophy, streetlights, water lines and other utilities were put into place before any residences were constructed. "We provide 40-foot parking alleys in the business district, waving adieus to the 'no parking signs,'" he stated in the April 10, 1926 issue of *This Week in Venice*. "We provide wide streets, Venice Avenue being 200 feet wide in the residence section. And Venice is giving the people a 6-inch concrete base on all their heavy-duty streets. Nearly one half the first unit is given to tennis courts, parks, boulevards, civic center, and other recreational and public space. It's easy to get this space now, but it would be impossible 10 years from now. Venice, incidentally, is being planned for 50 years ahead."

Along the beach, Nolen planned a linear park that would protect the dunes. The park would include an amphitheater that would offer the Gulf of Mexico as a backdrop. Nolen also planned and advocated for a 230-acre community to be built for African Americans he called Harlem Village. The plan called for three thousand people to be housed in two neighborhoods with single-family homes set on fifty-foot lots. Another five hundred people would be housed in apartments in the community's center. While other

Early view of West Venice Avenue looking west toward the residential section and the Gulf of Mexico, circa 1926. *Venice Historical Resources.*

Florida cities had rejected the idea of creating separate communities for blacks, the BLE was amenable to Nolen's vision. Unfortunately, neither Harlem Village nor the beachfront park ever materialized.

At the urging of George Webb, the BLE's man in charge of building Venice, Nolen designed a subdivision east of town that contained "some cheaper lots" that railroad pensioners could afford to buy. Called Edgewood, the plat was located east of the railroad tracks and industrial area and consisted of sixteen blocks arranged in a grid pattern. Building in Edgewood began in July 1926 when thirty houses were announced for construction with a combined value of $135,000. Some private builders purchased lots and constructed speculation houses, while others built houses for individual lot owners.

The modest houses were built on 50-by-150-foot lots with a mandatory set-back from the property line of 25 feet. This resulted in a uniform street appearance regardless of the building's design. Most were designed with elements of the Mediterranean Revival style, although architectural standards were not as strictly enforced as in other areas of the city under construction. Building materials also varied from one-story wood-frame structures to hollow clay tile or poured concrete with a smooth textured stucco finish. The homes were mass constructed, with as many as a half dozen constructed simultaneously by the same builder.

Promotional literature described Edgewood as a place where "the man of modest means can buy a homesite within five minutes' walk" of the city's business section. A special 10 percent discount was offered to BLE members with favorable financing terms. The offer was good through October 31, 1926. Empty lots ranged in price from $850 to $1,600.

A pragmatist with a Renaissance view of the world, Nolen believed that Venice, like every city, should be a dramatic, aesthetic experience. And it should be available to all its residents, regardless of their cultural or economic status. "Venice would be a place," he added, "where the ordinary man could have a chance to get all that the rich have ever been able to get out of Florida."

Nolen liked to establish review boards for all his projects in order to provide local feedback on his designs. Since Venice had no residents in the early stages of the city's development, and he was working remotely from his Cambridge, Massachusetts office, he encouraged the BLE to hire a fellow Harvard graduate, Prentiss French, to handle the town's landscaping and ensure that his plan was being correctly implemented.

French was born in Chicago in 1894 into an artistic family. His father directed the Chicago Art Museum for thirty years, and his uncle, Daniel Chester French, was a famous sculptor whose works included the *Minute Man at Concord* statue as well as the Lincoln Memorial in Washington, D.C. French

arrived in Venice in January 1926, along with Harold Heller, a fellow classmate, who skipped his Harvard graduation ceremony in order to start work in Venice right away. The two men took up residence in a newly constructed house in Nokomis built by Alvah Jordan, a wealthy businessman from Everett, Washington.

Upon his arrival, French organized and hired crews to begin clearing land in preparation for landscaping. He established a forty-acre nursery, complete with a ten-thousand-gallon water tank for irrigation, large shade houses, potting and storage sheds and a cottage for the superintendent. About a dozen men operated the nursery under the direction of F. Paul Horne, who also was responsible for landscaping John Ringling's estate in Sarasota.

Prentiss French, 1927. *Venice Historical Resources.*

Right: BLE Nursery Manager F. Paul Horne in front of the superintendent's cottage, 1926. *Venice Historical Resources.*

Below: Washington Palms in BLE's forty-acre nursery, 1926. *Venice Historical Resources.*

French imported thousands of trees and plants from as far away as Japan and Madagascar, while a staff of some fifty designers and plant men provided cut flowers and plants to local hotels. Three-fourths of all the trees and many plants were native to Florida, so they would grow well in the tropical environment.

The landscaping of resident homes was tightly controlled by the BLE. Individual builders were required to submit landscape plans before obtaining construction loans. The company also encouraged homeowners by allowing them to take advantage of French's landscape department while also financing the work. "That to me is very gratifying, because after all, a city in order to be beautiful, as a whole, must be made up of homes with individual beauty," he said in the June 3, 1927 edition of the *Venice News*. "I am greatly interested in individual beautification work, and our department is more than anxious to help our residents to plan and execute home planting schemes."

By May 1926, once the nursery was operating effectively, French focused his attention on planting citrus trees in the business district and live oaks along Venice Avenue. Inside the walled-in courtyard of the Hotel Venice, he placed orange trees with small illuminated orange globes strung throughout the branches. Nicknamed the Orange Grove, dances were held in the courtyard on Wednesday and Saturday nights, with music provided by the Anthony Lopez Orchestra.

By the fall of 1926, French had 4,770 trees, 3,800 shrubs and 1,450 vines in various states of growth. Nolen happily noted that landscaping was finally getting the attention in Venice it deserved. "Beautification work is, of course, a delight to all of us here in Florida, where the climate is so conducive to rapid and prolific growth," French said in the June 3, 1927 edition of *Venice News*. "There is such a variety of material to work with that it makes the task much easier than it would be in a colder climate."

For planners like Nolen and French, designing a utopian community like Venice was a lifetime opportunity to put into place everything they had learned at Harvard and experienced through their many previous projects. It validated their ideas of what constituted a better quality of life. "More and more people these days want more ideal living conditions if they can get them without needless expense," Nolen said in the June 1, 1926 edition of *This Week in Venice*. "They want schools, libraries, ample parkways and recreational space; architectural regulations that are a protection against 'atrocities,' lots large enough to have a little breathing space."

The promise of Venice, they believed, offered all that and more.

FLORIDA'S "FASTEST-GROWING CITY" TAKES SHAPE

When the BLE Realty leadership began construction of Venice in 1926, their priority was to create hotel space where potential buyers could stay while touring the state's newest city. Forcing visitors to seek accommodations in Nokomis and Sarasota did little to foster the vision of a utopia they were in the process of creating.

The first building to be constructed was the Hotel Venice, located at the corner of North Nassau Street and Tampa Avenue, one block from downtown Venice Boulevard (Avenue). The February 11, 1926 edition of *This Week in Sarasota* announced that the foundation for the three-story building had largely been completed. Constructed in the Mediterranean Renaissance style, the hotel boasted one hundred rooms, each equipped with "large windows, ventilating doors and ceiling fans in each room to ensure coolness at all times." Most rooms were available for five dollars per day, while the more spacious suites cost no more than fifteen dollars.

"Hotel Venice will not be the most expensive or pretentious hotel in Florida, but none will be more comfortable nor complete in its appointments," reported the June 26, 1926 edition of *This Week in Venice*.

Constructed at a cost of slightly less than $500,000, the hotel was completed in three months. A feature was the spacious ninety-by-eighty-five-foot patio that served as its grand entrance and was surrounded on three sides by the building. A fountain designed by Harold Heller graced the center of the patio and was interspersed with seats "designed for the pleasure of the guests." The patio was flanked by the hotel's two wings. The

Hotel Venice in 1926. *Venice Historical Resources.*

south wing housed the dining room, while the north wing was occupied by representatives of the Venice Company, the sales arm of BLE Realty.

Both the main lobby and the 150-seat dining room featured cypress-beamed ceilings and terrazzo floors. The hotel offered plenty of amenities, including its own bakery, laundry, and barbershop, as well as ice machines capable of producing two thousand pounds of ice per day. Located just outside the dining room was a walled courtyard nicknamed the Orange Grove. The courtyard was lined with orange trees provided by the city's landscape architect, Prentiss French, that were illuminated with small orange globes woven through the branches. Antonio Lopez and his Venice Orchestra performed for dances on Wednesday and Saturday nights. Guests were entertained the rest of the week through the French doors that lined the dining room.

It was constructed with a wood frame and stucco exterior, and many of the materials used were manufactured locally. Also, much of the food served at the Hotel Venice was grown locally at the nearby Venice Farms. And the hotel was decorated throughout with flowers and plants provided by Dr. Fred Albee's and the BLE's nurseries.

BLE Realty recruited some of the most experienced hospitality workers from throughout the country to operate the Hotel Venice. Charles P. Kane, former manager of the St. Francis Hotel in San Francisco as well as other fashionable hotels throughout the country, was hired to oversee the new enterprise. For the comfort and safety of its guests, the hotel was outfitted with elevators provided by the Otis Company and had an automatic fire sprinkler system installed throughout. Furnishings were of a Spanish style and were specially designed and built to order by the George Reinhard Company of New York City.

The Hotel Venice was formally opened to the public on June 21, 1926, and the dining room began serving meals eight days later. The hotel hosted prominent leaders in business, sports, entertainment, and politics. Thomas and Mina Edison, who wintered in Fort Myers, were known to have visited at least once. Perhaps most important, the hotel could host visitors to the growing city interested in purchasing a home or starting a business in Venice.

The Hotel Venice relieved some of the pressure for accommodations, but more was needed. George T. Webb, the BLE's vice-president in charge of

Dining room of Hotel Venice, 1926. *Tampa-Hillsborough County Library.*

the project, summoned his engineers to a meeting one evening to determine how more hotels could be built quickly. At the meeting, which reportedly lasted until 4:00 a.m. the following morning, he was told that it would take weeks to design plans for a new hotel. It was instead decided to build a second hotel using the exact same drawings for the Hotel Venice, except for an enclosed courtyard and a few other minor design changes. Construction began right away for the Park View Hotel, which was located at the corner of Venice Boulevard and Harbor Drive (present site of the Post Office). The Park View opened on February 11, 1927.

The city of Venice got an early Christmas present on December 10, 1926, when the San Marco Hotel along Tampa Avenue formally opened its doors to the public. The second of three hotels built by the BLE, the three-story hotel that encompassed the entire city block in the center of town was described in an August edition of *This Week in Venice* as "one of the most beautiful yet planned for Venice."

Constructed at a cost of $300,000 and completed in just three months, the San Marco featured a modern steam heating system with radiators in each of its ninety-two rooms. The December 10, 1926 edition of the *Venice News* also mentioned that the hotel featured patented water softening equipment for the comfort of its guests.

Also designed in the Venetian architectural style, the San Marco differed from the city's other buildings in that it was constructed of concrete block, covered with stucco and reinforced with steel columns. The hotel's owner, R.W. Wishart, was a widely known contractor at the time and was responsible for much of the development on Davis Island in Tampa. Plumbing, electrical work and furnishings were provided by various Tampa-based contractors, and the elevators were also provided by the Otis Company. E.E. Allen of New York furnished the linens.

"Everybody in town knew that the hotel was strong," said Julia Cousins-Laning, who moved with her family to Venice when she was six years old, about the time the San Marco was built. "Whenever bad weather threatened the area, local families would be invited to stay there to ride out the storm. We children would run up and down the hallways, gathering the little soaps and shampoos."

Space on the ground floor was reserved for thirteen offices and retail shops. Included in the initial offering was a barbershop, a dentist, insurance and real estate offices, as well as a retail shop selling a variety of merchandise and offering a rental library. A local physician, Dr. W.C. Page, operated his practice from there, and a Western Union telegraph office was also located

Park View Hotel, sister building of the Hotel Venice, 1926. *Venice Historical Resources.*

San Marco Hotel, circa 1927. *Venice Historical Resources.*

in the building. A café was at the eastern end of the building. And two lobbies with working fireplaces were located at each end.

An advertisement in the February 6, 1930 edition of the *Sarasota Herald Tribune* stated that rooms in the San Marco were available for three dollars per day, each available with bath.

A fourth resort hotel to be built near Casey's Pass, offering a splendid view of both the Gulf and the surrounding bays, was planned by Nolen but never built. The February 11, 1927 edition of the *Venice News* noted that even with the three completed hotels, "The need for hotel accommodations is still heavily in excess of the supply." With a residential population of 3,500 and a daily visiting list of 500 transients, there was continuing pressure to increase the number of available beds.

Smaller hotels were built to accommodate visitors. The two-story Venezia Hotel was built to the east and across the street from the San Marco and opened in February 1927. Constructed by C. Franklyn Wheeler of Fort Myers, the hotel offered fifty-six rooms. The month before, the Hotel Valencia and Ennes Arcade Building was completed. Located at 229 West Venice Boulevard, the two-story building cost $125,000 to construct and consisted of two buildings facing each other that were connected on the first floor by a roofed, open-ended arcade.

The hotel and arcade complex were constructed for Stanton and Elizabeth Ennes. Mr. Ennes served as general manager of the BLE's Venice Company from September 1927 until March 1928.

Seven stores, besides the hotel lobby and post office, occupied the first floor, with some opening directly onto the arcade. By July 1927, the building housed the Turner Clothing Store, the Arcade Barber Shop, the Prime Hardware Company, the Venice News Company, and an office of the Florida Power & Light Company. Facing the street on the building's right side was the Venice Café, which would later serve as the location for the Dick & Meadows Pharmacy. The November 25, 1930 edition of the *Sarasota Herald* included a café advertisement offering a sumptuous Thanksgiving dinner for just seventy-five cents.

The Valencia Hotel, which was located on the second floor of the building, offered thirty-two rooms with sixteen shared bathrooms. Each room opened to an outside second-story patio, while the hotel's lobby was located on the first floor, to the left of the arcade. Living quarters for the proprietor's family was located just behind the lobby, with the city's post office located at the south end of the building. There was no home delivery at that time. Instead, each resident was issued a post office box where they went to retrieve their

Valencia Hotel and Arcade, circa 1927. *Venice Historical Resources.*

mail. The first-floor offices were eventually converted to retail shops and the upstairs hotel into apartments. But the Valencia Hotel and Ennes Building has continued to serve as a hub for the historic Venice community.

While the number of available beds for visitors continued to increase, Venice's commercial district was also beginning to take shape. BLE Realty encouraged successful businessmen from throughout Florida, but especially along the Gulf Coast, to set up shop in the planned community.

The two-story Boissevain Building, the town's first commercial building, began construction in May 1926 and was located at 205 Venice Boulevard. Two retail stores were located on the bottom floor, while a billiard parlor was planned for upstairs.

The Johnson-Schoolcraft Building occupied the southwest corner of Venice Boulevard and Nokomis Avenue. Venice's first pharmacy filled the first floor, while five apartments were located upstairs. The Peninsular Telephone Company operated its switchboard from a rear office. In case of an emergency, residents would notify the telephone operator, who would turn on a red light on top of the building, thereby alerting police to contact the operator for details on who needed their help.

In 1927, Dr. Fred Albee, who had founded the Venice-Nokomis Bank in Nokomis just two years before, constructed a new $75,000 building at the northwest corner of Venice Boulevard and Nassau Street. And next door to it, Newport Estes of Orlando built a complex of buildings covering four lots

Above: Johnson-Schoolcraft Building, 1926. *Venice Historical Resources.*

Opposite, top: Venice-Nokomis Bank Building under construction, 1927. *Venice Historical Resources.*

Opposite, bottom: The Green Building on the corner of Miami and Ponce de Leon, 1926. *Venice Historical Resources.*

that included the city's first movie theater. The Park View Hotel was located at the far west end of the block.

In addition to the activity on Venice Boulevard, four buildings were under construction on Miami Avenue. Thomas Green, a businessman from St. Petersburg, constructed the triangular-shaped building at the intersection of Miami and Ponce de Leon Avenues at a cost of $85,000. Designed by Harrison Gill, the first architect to locate in Venice, the two-story building was modeled after the iconic Flat Iron building in New York City and was described as of Spanish design due to its clay tile and stucco over brick construction.

The Green Building contained ten apartments upstairs, five stores, four offices and an arcade-like automotive garage at the eastern end of the building. Tenants included hardware and sporting goods stores, as well as spray paint and electrical shops.

The July 10, 1926 edition of *This Week in Venice* stated that Green was "very pleased at the prospect of business in Venice. He has purchased a five-acre farm just outside the city limits, which he expects to live on and cultivate himself." The article added that while Green was not giving up his business interests in St. Petersburg, he expected to devote most of his time to his enterprises in Venice.

Located west of the Green Building was the Wimmers Building, named for its first owner and tenant, H.N. "Bud" Wimmers, who served as paymaster for the BLE Realty work crews that were constructing Venice. Considered one of the city's founding fathers, he later served as a councilman and receiver for the BLE's affairs after the union pulled out of the project. Wimmers became a prominent real estate broker in town, as well as served as representative for the area's power, telephone, telegraph and water services.

To the west was the Teal Building, which was constructed by L.M. Teal and housed the Teal Barber Shop and Venice Billiard Hall. It later served as an elementary school, funeral home and automotive garage.

The last building on the block, also constructed in 1926, was the Lawton Building, named for Mrs. Louis L. Lawton of St. Petersburg. The one-story retail building was designed by Harrison Gill and constructed at a cost of $15,000 by Carey & Walter of Plant City. The architectural style was unique,

Business section of Venice showing Venice and Miami Avenues, circa 1930. *Venice Historical Resources.*

with front doors set back from the storefront windows so that the display areas appeared as bay windows, also protecting shoppers from the elements. Seven shops occupied the one-hundred-foot-long building.

By the late fall of 1925, the first subdivision, called the Gulf View Section of Venice, was platted and ready for filing. Planner John Nolen wanted each section of town to have its own distinctive "look" while remaining true to the overall plan. Most of these homes were built by private contractors, either on speculation or by contract. Adhering to the Mediterranean style of architecture, all plans were reviewed by the New York City architectural firm of Walker and Gillette and the company's on-site representative, Howard Patterson. To encourage sales, the Venice Company announced in July 1926 that the BLE had made available a $6 million loan fund to offer financial aid to Venice buyers.

Nolen understood that if Venice was to be sustainable as a community, there needed to be affordable housing in the form of apartments. A collection of multi-family dwellings was constructed in the "Armada Road District." Tampa builder M.G. Worrell constructed ten apartment buildings at a cost of $38,000 each.

Ground was broken on September 20, 1927, for the first cluster of fourteen apartments on Palmetto Court. Built by the Venice Investment Company and designed by Harrison Gill, the apartments were divided into five- and six-room units and cost a reported $78,000 to construct, with an additional $25,000 spent on furnishings.

According to articles published in the fall 1927 editions of the *Venice News*, a promotional contest was held to formally name these "bungalow court" apartments. The contest concluded on October 17, and the winner of the twenty-five-dollar first-place prize was announced on November 3, with the apartments named "La Casa Bonita," which translated as the beautiful home. The complex was later renamed the Granada Apartments, reflecting their Spanish Colonial design.

The Triangle Inn, located at the corner of South Nassau Street and Pensacola Road, was also built in 1927 as a two-story rooming house or inn. Mrs. Augusta Miner, who previously had operated a tearoom in Chicago, lived in the inn she had built and continued to operate it as a lodging until 1934. The building was eventually acquired by the City of Venice in 1991 and moved two blocks south to 351 South Nassau Street. Following the building's refurbishment, the Triangle Inn houses the city's historic museum and offices of the Division of Historic Resources.

Apartment buildings constructed by M.G. Worrell on Armada Road, circa 1927. *Venice Historical Resources.*

Triangle Inn, originally located at 251 Nassau Street South, circa 1935. *Venice Historical Resources.*

View of 519 South Harbor Drive, known today as the Banyan House, circa 1927. *Venice Historical Resources.*

In addition to the Gulf View section, Nolen also platted the Venezia Park subdivision, which was distinctive not only for the architectural merits of the middle-class homes that were built there but also for the unique pattern of the streets and parks comprising the district. The subdivision was roughly bounded by Palermo, Sorrento and Salerno Streets, as well as Harbor Drive to the west. The city's golf course was located to the east and within walking distance.

Many elegant residences were constructed throughout the district. Perhaps one of the most iconic was the house at 519 South Harbor Drive, more commonly known today as the Banyan House. Built in 1926, the six-bedroom, five-bathroom home was constructed for Bob and Dorothy Marvin. A trained engineer, Bob Marvin oversaw the sale of private residences for the Venice Company. The fourteen-room residence, finished with imported pink marble floors, featured three fireplaces—two on the first floor and one in the upstairs master bedroom. The exterior consisted of double-hollow tile faced with brick and covered with stucco. The design not only protected the home from severe weather but also offered some relief during the hot summers.

Venice Tile Company, 1926.
Venice Historical Resources.

Thomas Edison was a friend of the Marvins and would stay with them during visits to Venice. He gave the family a banyan tree in 1928 that was planted next to the house, thus giving the residence its nickname. Over the years, in addition to serving as a residence, the house also served as a preschool, a shell museum, a USO facility and as a bed-and-breakfast.

To support all the construction taking place in Venice, the industrial area located east of the city and south of the Seaboard train depot also expanded rapidly. Some forty companies established operations there. One of the first and largest was the Venice Tile Company, which manufactured distinctive "old mission" roof tile, floor and decorative materials. Other companies included lumber companies, concrete products and other hardware and building material companies. The Woodcrafters of Venice made toys and other novelties of hand-painted wood. And the Venice Novelty Works, a manufacturer of sash and doors as well as other millwork, was established by Grounds Brothers of St. Petersburg.

"There are two essentials for the development of an industrial center other than location, power, and transportation," stated the June 3, 1927 edition of the *Venice News*. "Those are raw material and labor." The article went on to state that Venice possessed both of those necessities in abundance, thereby ensuring its growing importance in the new industrial South.

VENICE FARMS

W hile development of the city of Venice continued at a rapid pace, BLE Realty was also working feverishly to transform the twenty-five thousand acres of fertile land east to the Myakka River into Venice Farms.

In an article published in the May 30, 1926 edition of the *Tampa Tribune*, George T. Webb, the vice-president in charge of the project, said that developing the agricultural program was the most important component for creating the city's sustainability. "Commerce and industry, and their handmate, transportation, will quickly follow intensive agricultural production," he added.

While executives saw the city of Venice as a magnet for wealthy northerners looking for the ideal winter playground, Venice Farms, they reasoned, would provide a lucrative revenue stream during the off-season.

Of course, BLE Realty was not the first to recognize the potential for turning this undeveloped scrub into highly productive farmland. Joseph Lord, who at one time owned a majority of what would become South Sarasota County, sought to attract investors at the turn of the twentieth century. He captured the attention in 1910 of Bertha Honoré Palmer, who purchased some 140,000 acres of land, much of which was turned into lucrative farm and ranch land. And Dr. Fred Albee also created his Albee Farms, which was noted for growing and shipping fruit and gladiolus bulbs to northern markets.

Advertisement for Venice Farms, 1927. *From the* Venice News.

Several factors contributed to the area's agricultural success. First, the semitropical environment provided ideal growing conditions, allowing for vegetable crops to mature in one hundred days or fewer. Also, the soil contained high concentrations of phosphate, a primary ingredient in fertilizer—that and the fact that the sandy soil allowed for favorable drainage.

The Venice Farms plan followed the model implemented by the Palmer Company in Sarasota more than a decade before by creating five- and ten-acre farms. The sales pitch to potential farmers was as follows: thanks to the rich soil and ideal climate conditions, at least two yields could be grown during a normal growing season.

"The winter farmer at Venice Farms puts in just about six months of the year planting, cultivating, and harvesting his 'money crops' of winter-grown fruit and vegetables for the northern markets," boasted an advertisement in the *Venice News*. "The rest of the year is his own. He has ample leisure time to enjoy all the thousand and one things there are to do at this wonderful new resort city on the Gulf."

Prior to sale, each of the farm sites was cleared, drained, fenced, plowed and disked. Although the area reportedly enjoyed an average fifty inches of rainfall per year, several artesian wells were dug to ensure needed irrigation. And a cover crop was planted before each farm site was sold.

In his original design for Venice, city planner John Nolen called for a one-hundred-foot-wide boat channel to extend from Venice (Roberts) Bay east through the Venice Farms and connect with the Myakka River. Nolen's plan for the Intracoastal Waterway, which would have provided a water route to the Peace River and eventual access to Charlotte Harbor, was never realized.

In just ninety days, hundreds of laborers built a twelve-mile, hard surface Venice Farms Road (presently East Venice Avenue) to facilitate transporting crops to the Train Depot for shipment as well as to local city markets.

Horace K. Haldeman helped BLE Realty oversee Venice Farms development. In a June 3, 1927 edition of the *Venice News*, he stated that the first crops had been planted the previous July but that no real effort toward production occurred until the 1927 spring crop. "From his spring crop, one farmer has shipped two carloads of early potatoes, six cars of tomatoes, and three cars of early watermelons to date, showing what can be done."

Haldeman went on to say that the first section of farm sites, consisting of about 1,500 acres, was already about 95 percent cleared and 75 percent either in crop or cover crop. The intent of those in charge was to prepare in advance the land for a prospective buyer, as well as to provide assistance as to what, when and where to plant, he said.

A new home in the BLE Venice Farms, circa 1926. *Venice Historical Resources.*

Venice Farms advertised that a typical ten-acre parcel sold for $450 per acre and was suitable for growing a variety of cash crops such as peppers, potatoes, eggplants, watermelons, squash, peas, beans, cucumbers, and strawberries. Along with the cost of purchasing farm equipment, a small furnished house and barn, as well as a few other expenses, it was estimated that a farmer could go into business for about $10,000.

BLE Realty set aside eighty acres of land to serve as experimental demonstration farms. Albert Blackburn, a third-generation settler who had served as a ranch foreman for Bertha Palmer and later helped BLE Realty acquire its land in Venice, was placed in charge of the farm tracts. He reported in a 1926 edition of *This Week in Venice* that planting first started on July 15 and that "tomatoes would be the chief crop with a few acres of squash and potatoes."

Blackburn went on to say that "we have been talking a lot about what Venice Farm land will do, and now we are going to do some showing. The soil is very fertile, we know, because we have obtained some wonderful results on our nursery stuff."

In addition to the four demonstration farms, Venice Farms created a ten-acre strawberry demonstration farm, a model dairy farm and a five-acre poultry demonstration farm carrying thirty thousand chickens.

BLE demonstration farm cutting and boxing celery for market, 1926. *Venice Historical Resources.*

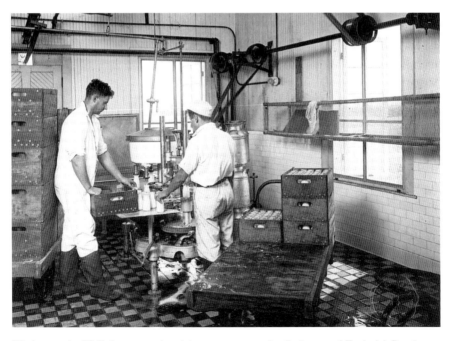

Workers at the BLE demonstration dairy near present-day Jackson and Frederick Roads, 1926. *Venice Historical Resources.*

Haldeman reported that the entire 160-acre dairy farm was fenced and cross-fenced into 25-acre plots that were cleared and seeded to crops. The operation began with a herd of 140 Guernsey and Jersey cows and 4 Guernsey bulls. The well-lit and ventilated dairy barn had a capacity for milking up to 300 cows in three relays.

Like the homes and businesses it promoted, the Venice Company launched a nationwide public relations campaign touting the success of Venice Farms. An entire September 1926 edition of *Florida Grower Magazine* featured the many benefits of farming in Venice, while the Associated Press carried numerous articles describing its "assured success" operation. One advertisement asked the question, "Wouldn't you rather be on a Venice Farm, where a good income from the production of winter-grown fruits and vegetables is easily supplemented by the sale of milk and cream from a few dairy cows?"

The promotional campaigns succeeded, and several families, including some with no real farming experience, invested in the vision. Unfortunately, that vision didn't fit with reality. Many soon realized that the farm tracts weren't large enough to provide a sustainable income. And the claims about

Manhattan Produce Exchange storage building for fruit and vegetables being shipped to Tampa, 1926. *Venice Historical Resources.*

the ideal growing environment didn't always meet expectations. As the economy stumbled and sales dwindled, "For Sale" signs began to appear by owners anxious to get out.

During the 1930s, after the Brotherhood had abandoned the Venice project, a number of small farmers as well as large agricultural companies farmed the area. "Packing houses have been built by several of the largest farming interests, and Venice has made a step toward becoming a marketing center for growers in adjacent territories," reported the November 12, 1939 edition of the *Tampa Daily Times*.

Companies such as the Stone Farms of New York and the Albee Farms in Nokomis planted acres of citrus fruit. One Florida firm, the John S. Barnes Company, purchased 1,500 acres, while W.C. Spencer Jr. of Tampa planted some 400 acres of crops such as cucumbers, tomatoes and potatoes.

Another substantial grower in the area was the Manhattan Produce Exchange, which used as its packinghouse a 5,800-square-foot building, originally constructed in 1928, adjacent to the Venice Train Depot for the purpose of storing luggage and freight. Venice native Glenn Stephens worked as a young man for the company sorting cucumbers in preparation for shipment to northern markets. After the vegetables were unloaded at the eastern side of the building and graded by size and quality, he said they were then moved by hand trucks through large doors on the western side of the building and onto the refrigerated freight cars.

"The cars were refrigerated by large blocks of ice, weighing several hundred pounds, that were produced by the ice plant in Nokomis," Stephens said. "They would back the truck up to the railroad car and put a block and tackle on top of the boxcar and then run the rope down with the ice tongs. Once the driver had pulled the rope tight, he'd drive the truck out from under the block of ice. He'd then chip the block into smaller pieces. With the wind passing over the ice and through the train car, that's how they kept the produce fresh until it reached northern markets."

An article in the *Tampa Daily Times* reported that the company was shipping three carloads daily of cucumbers of the highest grade grown in Florida to the markets.

THE END OF THE DREAM

W hile construction in Venice continued at breakneck pace throughout 1926, financial storm clouds were forming, both in Southwest Florida and at the Brotherhood of Locomotive Engineers (BLE) headquarters in Cleveland, Ohio. Potential buyers were becoming nervous by growing signs that the nation's economy might be weakening. And the Great Miami Hurricane in September 1926, which caused millions in damages and took hundreds of lives across South Florida, virtually ended the state's land boom that had begun years earlier.

"Blooie—and the bubble of Florida real estate promotion collapsed overnight," said one union official. "The roads were clogged with autos seeking to escape the ruins. Grass began to grow on the 'streets' of million-dollar promotions. The real estate gentry escaped Florida in a flood, which swamped all the Pullmans which could be rushed from the North. And there was Venice—disconsolate by the waters. Millions sunk in the city, millions more to be sunk before a penny could be realized."

Despite the warning signs, the promotional material cranked out by the Venice Company, the sales arm of the BLE Realty Company, continued to assure potential buyers that the building of Venice was a project simply too big to fail. At every opportunity, sales representatives reminded potential buyers that the nation's largest union had committed millions to the project. As one advertisement stated that thanks to "backing by enormous resources," completion of "this giant undertaking" was virtually assured. By the beginning of 1926, the Venice Company had sold about $2 million worth

Warren Stanford Stone, circa 1916. *Wikimedia Commons.*

of property, and by the summer of that year, the total had reached $4.5 million. Most of those sales, however, were on the deferred payment plan through loans provided with union money.

By the end of the 1926–27 tourist season, sales were but a mere fraction of what they had been a year earlier. Curious visitors stopped coming and interest waned. By March 1927, BLE Realty was forced to limit Fuller Construction expenses to just $30,000 per week, down from a reported $1 million spent per month at the beginning of the project. As a result, Fuller began laying off its workforce and construction slowed.

The labor banking movement got its start in 1920, when the Brotherhood launched the Cooperative National Bank in Cleveland, Ohio. The bank's resources totaled some $27 million in just two years. Backed with confidence, the Brotherhood would become the predominant investor in more than a dozen banks nationwide. The Brotherhood's grand chief engineer, Warren S. Stone, once boasted that it was as easy to operate a bank as it was a peanut stand. Union members would soon come to rue the folly of that statement.

Due to the lavish spending, the Venice project was putting a strain on the union's financial strength. By the late summer, the BLE had sold its bank in New York City, with the organization's investment in the Empire Trust Company soon to follow.

By March 1927, the union's corporate lawyers were warning then BLE President William Prenter that the organization was in grave financial danger and that it needed to take corrective action quickly. The lawyers pointed out that BLE Realty executives provided no estimate on how much more funding the Florida venture needed. In effect, the union had given BLE Realty officers a blank check with which to build the resort city.

The growing tension came to a head on June 6, 1927, when the Brotherhood held its triennial convention in Cleveland. A "committee of ten" investigators was formed to assess the financial operations of BLE Realty as well as other speculative ventures. The committee noted that the Venice project had originally been created to conceal the loss of $4 million in a previous investment gone sour and that operating losses by BLE Realty had surpassed that amount in just its first sixteen months of operation. The report also revealed that the salaries of some of the BLE Realty executives amounted to as much as four times that of the average union member, who earned about twenty-nine dollars per week. When the committee's findings began to leak out publicly, panic ensued, and many of the union's creditors began to demand payment.

According to *The Labor Banking Movement in the United States*, published in 1929 by Princeton University Press, "The huge losses, error of judgement, betrayals of confidence, nepotism, inefficiency, and extravagance that permeated the financial system, which had so long camouflaged itself as a great and glorious enterprise, were brought home suddenly to the bewildered delegates."

The convention in Cleveland lasted from June 6 until July 21, the longest ever held by the union, and at a cost of about $1 million. The committee stunned delegates with what they had uncovered in their two-thousand-page report: through greed and mismanagement, the Brotherhood had been thrust into one of the greatest financial disasters in American history. As William Foster concluded in his case study on how the Brotherhood "wrecked" the labor banks, "their trusted and 'brilliant' leaders they found to be charlatans and grafters when not incredibly stupid and incompetent."

Earlier in 1927, Prenter and Florida Governor John Martin had welcomed delegates to Venice. Governor Martin told them that he saw Venice as "the dawn of a new era of prosperity, which will resound to the credit of the city, the state, and the nation." Just months later in Cleveland, however, with a clearer picture of the financial challenges before them, delegates voted to get out of the Venice project and to fire Prenter and three other union executives who had misled them regarding the severity of the project's dire financial problems.

Alvanley Johnston, a railroader who had risen through the ranks, was put in charge of the union. Claudius Huston, chairman of Transcontinental Oil and later head of the Republican National Committee, was brought in to manage the union's financial affairs. And a group of Cleveland-based businessmen replaced the BLE's investment board.

In summarizing their investigation, the committee of ten, now reduced to eight, concluded that the union has "been buffeted about in the financial world and have been the prey of promoters whose weird schemes have rocked our very foundation." And with respect to the Venice project, "we cannot help but reach the conclusion that this venture was nothing more nor less

Above: Governor John Martin and BLE President W.B. Prentor, 1925. *Venice Historical Resources.*

Opposite, top: H.N. "Bud" Wimmers, circa 1926. *Venice Historical Resources.*

Opposite, middle: The Albees, circa 1930. *Venice Historical Resources.*

Opposite, bottom: The first mayor of Venice, Edward "Ned" Worthington, 1926. *Venice Historical Resources.*

than downright stupidity." By the end of 1927, the amount owed various creditors amounted to more than $14 million. No accounting of the actual losses on the project was ever made public.

In 1928, Florida Power & Light purchased the city's private electrical distribution system for $150,000. H.N. "Bud" Wimmers, who had come to Venice as assistant treasurer and paymaster for the project in 1926, remained behind to serve as "receiver" for BLE Realty properties and to try to liquidate as much of the company's remaining assets as possible. The BLE Realty Corporation and the Venice Company faced dozens of lawsuits, whose legal entanglements would continue for decades.

Since Dr. Fred Albee had originally sold the land for Venice to BLE Realty and still held the paper on much of it, with ownership reverting to him. Albee later wrote that when the bubble finally burst and the BLE "stopped spending money, the artificially stimulated prosperity of the city ceased and Venice became a ghost town."

Stanton Ennes, former general manager of BLE Realty, published a book in 1929, *The Locomotive Engineers Investment in Florida Real Estate, Venice*, in which he blamed much of the failure of the Venice project on mismanagement, particularly that of Vice-President George T. Webb. "You wouldn't want to ride behind an engineer who learned his railroading in a bank, and for the same reason, you shouldn't trust your savings to men who got their financial training on a locomotive," he said.

E. L. Worthington

By the end of 1927, BLE Realty holdings in Venice amounted to some fifty-three thousand acres, including eighty square miles of undeveloped land. Ennes said that as it became increasingly evident that there were more sellers than buyers, BLE Realty worked that much harder at promoting the project.

Edward L. "Ned" Worthington, who served as vice-president and treasurer of the Venice Company, had previously run a brokerage firm in Cleveland. In addition to his role as an executive with BLE Realty, Worthington and his wife, Ann, became the largest individual landowners in Venice and invested in the construction of the Worthington Apartments. By an act of the 1925 Florida legislature, Governor Martin appointed Worthington mayor of the town of Venice, effective the following year. On May 4, 1927, the legislature changed the status of Venice from a town to a city. The city collected a total of $94,926 in ad valorem and personal taxes in 1927 on an appraised value of $9,492,667. In 1928, however, it collected only $73,151 in taxes. Venice's glory days were clearly in the rear-view mirror.

As Venice's future appeared increasingly bleak, life in the city put up a good front. Residents with means continued to dance away their concerns in the Hotel Venice's Orange Grove, while sportsmen chased after tarpon in the nearby bays and Gulf. The Venice Company continued to promote the city with advertising touting "One Hundred Things to Do at Venice."

Meanwhile, leadership of the Brotherhood attempted to minimize the financial damage to the nation's largest union. Johnston took over leadership of the ninety-one-thousand-member union, a position he would hold until 1950. The organization's financial affairs were turned over to Huston. And Thomas J. Bissett, a BLE Securities Corporation director, was put in charge of the Venice project.

Venice held its first city election in December 1927, with Mayor Worthington running unopposed for reelection. His last recorded official action occurred in April 1928, when he welcomed to the city a motorcade celebrating the opening of the recently completed Tamiami Trail. He, Ann and their two children left for Cleveland shortly thereafter, having lost virtually all in their Florida investments. He submitted his formal resignation as mayor on December 26, 1928.

To recoup some of the millions lost by the BLE Realty Corporation, the Brotherhood, at the 1927 convention, voted to raise $10 million by issuing $100 certificates of indebtedness called "Loyalty Loans." Representatives also voted to assess fifty-seven thousand union members, those who were active members prior to January 1927, an amount of $5 per month for two years. Many union members lost their entire life savings. Said one delegate to the convention, "Some years ago a man came out here on this platform [Stone] and said that banking was just as easy as running a peanut stand and, by God boys, that's the way that she has been run."

One of the vacant homes in Venice at 517 Menendez Street, no date. *Venice Historical Resources.*

Other posh cities in Florida like Coral Gables, Palm Beach and Belleaire also were experiencing the tightening of purse strings. But the belief among many in Venice, like other cities, was to simply hunker down and persevere until the economy recovered.

That dream ended, however, in October 1929 when the stock market crashed, plunging the country into the Great Depression. Banks closed their doors, businesses shuttered and families who had invested their life savings in the Venice dream loaded what they could into their cars and quietly left town with no forwarding address. Many homes remained furnished with whatever people left behind. A few families would remain to survive by whatever means they could.

Ennes, whom the BLE brought back to serve as general manager of BLE Realty, announced in the April 29, 1929 edition of the *Sarasota Herald*, "The Venice project where the Brotherhood of Locomotive Engineers endeavored to create a large city is now closed down indefinitely, lacking funds to continue." At the end of that year's season, Ennes observed that while every hotel in Florida was taxed to capacity, the one remaining Venice hotel still in operation had less than one floor filled. "The only apparent interest Venice now has for visitors is one of curiosity. They want to view the scene of the Brotherhood's failure in Florida. They want to see the wreck."

In their 1928 report to the Brotherhood leadership, the committee of eight concluded, "Had the enterprises we are engaged in been handled honestly, and with only a small degree of intelligence, we today would stand abreast of the world's greatest institutions."

Ennes continued to look for ways to slash costs. With construction at a standstill, Fuller Company workers left town in search of jobs elsewhere. And many BLE Realty employees were laid off as well. The engineering department, which at one time had employed more than one hundred men, was now reduced to fewer than a dozen.

At the BLE's triennial convention in June 1930, it was recommended that BLE Realty Corporation either file for bankruptcy or go into receivership. The company went into receivership at the end of 1931, along with the Seaboard Airline Railway and the Atlantic Coastline Railroad. The July 18, 1930 edition of the *New York Times* announced, "The Brotherhood of Locomotive Engineers will continue to hold and operate its $15,000,000 real estate investment at Venice, Florida until its financial chiefs can work out an acceptable plan of liquidation, it was announced [July 17] as the 1930 convention of the organization came to an end."

At the peak of development in 1926, a reported 3,500 people resided in Venice, with hundreds more visiting weekly. The 1930 census reported only 309 residents. The city turned off streetlights on moonlit nights to save electricity. Police and garbage collection was suspended. Wimmers said that homeowners at the time would get rid of what garbage they had by digging a hole in the backyard. And one old-timer recalled hunting rabbits on West Venice Avenue, where the grass was growing up through the pavement.

James Blalock, no date. *Venice Historical Resources.*

Truckloads of palm trees, once destined to line Venice's picturesque streets, went instead to Edward Bok's Singing Tower, which was under construction near Lake Wales.

In 1929, Jim Tom Blalock, cashier of the Venice-Nokomis Bank, became the second mayor of Venice. The thirty-two-year-old Blalock would go on to serve the city for a dozen years in that capacity. As for his employer, the bank started by Albee was one of the few in Florida that refused to close during the Depression.

By 1930, the city of Venice was badly bruised but still in the proverbial ring. The Brotherhood of Locomotive Engineers left the Venice project in financial failure. In its wake, however, was the start of a grand idea realized. In addition to its three vacant hotels, hundreds of residences and apartment buildings and more than eighty storefronts, Venice had more than a dozen paved roads, fifteen miles of sidewalks and twenty miles of curbing.

One old-timer, born in 1927 and whose father worked for BLE Realty, said that life in those early Depression years was difficult and that one had to work hard in order to survive. But those families who remained behind did so, he said, because they still saw the area as a land of opportunity. Wimmers would later say why he remained in Venice: "Hell, I can starve to death with pleasure here." He recalled going to where the jetty is located today to fish and "not return until I had caught the family's dinner for that evening." With no source of local income, he said that most families subsisted on whatever they could fish or hunt.

THE DAY THE KMI SPECIAL
CAME TO TOWN

They were not exactly the cavalry, but it must have seemed like it when the first trainload of cadets, instructors, and staff of the Kentucky Military Institute (KMI) rolled into the Venice Train Depot on January 5, 1933. An estimated 1,500 Suncoast residents, some from as far away as Sarasota and Fort Myers, converged on the special train at about 5:00 p.m. to welcome the school and the financial support it offered the beleaguered city.

Founded in 1845 in Frankfort, Kentucky, KMI was the oldest military school of its kind in the nation. It also was one of the first secondary schools in the country to affiliate with the U.S. Army's Reserve Officer Training Corps (ROTC) program.

More than eleven thousand boys matriculated at the military preparatory school during its 126-year history and went on to distinguish themselves in all walks of life. Alumni bravely served in all wars, up to and including Vietnam. Although military service was not a prerequisite following graduation, many alumni did choose to serve the nation in uniform. Seven generals during the Civil War were KMI graduates—five for the Union and two for the Confederacy.

Other distinguished alumni include nineteenth-century writer and journalist Ambrose Bierce, actors Victor Mature and Jim Backus, television comedian Fred Willard and Indianapolis race car driver Danny Sullivan.

KMI was founded by Colonel Robert T. Allen. He was a West Point graduate and distinguished army officer who also was an inventor and former college professor. The school was chartered in 1847 by the State of Kentucky and was to be operated as a quasi-military corps of the Commonwealth. Like other military institutes throughout the South at the time, KMI was to serve as a military training adjunct to the state's militia. This model would continue until the early nineteenth century, when the curriculum shifted from military science to one more focused on professional occupations.

Colonel Charles Fowler, an 1878 graduate of KMI, purchased the school in 1894 and moved it to a former plantation in Lyndon, Kentucky, a suburb of Louisville. Believing that outdoor recreation would benefit the cadets in their scholastic work, Fowler established a winter campus for the school in 1906 in Eau Gallie, Florida, located near Melbourne. The entire school would arrive shortly after the Christmas holiday break and would return to its Kentucky campus shortly before the Easter recess. The annual trip for the winter season continued until January 1920, when several buildings on the Florida campus were destroyed by fire. Because of that and a separate fire on the Kentucky campus, the school was forced into bankruptcy.

Four instructors from the Greenbriar Military School, led by Colonel Charles B. Richmond, purchased and reopened KMI in 1924 with an enrollment of 150 cadets. Like Fowler, Richmond also believed in the positive effects of the Florida climate and began searching for another winter campus.

In the late spring of 1932, Sarasota resident Ray Richardson, who had graduated from KMI in 1906 and had served as the school's commandant in 1909–10, contacted Richmond and informed him of the two vacant hotels in Venice, the Hotel Venice and the San Marco Hotel, that might serve as a suitable winter campus. Richmond arrived in Venice on a scouting expedition later that spring. Accompanied by representatives of the BLE Realty Corporation and the Seaboard Airline Railroad, he reportedly saw only three cars on the streets in Venice, one of which was "fixin' to leave."

Richmond was pleased with what he saw. He told a local reporter that he could not have designed the two Venice hotels better to serve as KMI's new winter campus, complete with twenty-five well-lit repurposed classrooms on the first floor of the San Marco.

The banner headline in the June 1, 1932 edition of the *Sarasota Herald-Tribune* announced the good news to a long-depressed Suncoast—exciting times were on the way. The paper noted that Richmond was, at that very moment, in meetings at the Brotherhood of Locomotive Engineers (BLE) headquarters in Cleveland to sign a nine-year lease on the two vacant buildings. His decision to bring KMI to Venice, he said, was influenced by

From left to right: James Cousins in his KMI uniform, Julia Cousins and father Mitt Cousins, circa 1933. *Venice Historical Resources.*

the availability of local fresh vegetables and modern rooms, as well as the beautiful nearby beach, a nine-hole golf course, notable land suitable for a parade ground and, of course, perfect chamber of commerce weather.

In announcing the news, the paper noted, "KMI at Venice is the beginning of a new era of prosperity." Bud Wimmers, who was left behind as the appointed receiver for the BLE's holdings in Venice, said that the announcement was "like a shot of adrenaline to a fellow with a heart condition."

For three months before KMI's arrival, work began to prepare the hotels, which had been closed for years. Furniture was "borrowed" from nearby vacated homes. Rosa Lee Smith was one of about six African American workers who were paid eleven dollars per week to clean the rooms. The cleaning crew was under the direction of Carmen Cousins, the wife of the building contractor and future Venice Mayor Mitt Cousins, who also was hired by KMI to maintain the winter campus.

The first "KMI Special," consisting of five sleepers and a baggage car, left Kentucky with about 175 boys, averaging sixteen years of age, as well as some of the 25 faculty members and administrators and 25 staff members. The train arrived from Louisville about forty hours later at the Venice Train Depot. The faculty, staff and cadets were met by an enthusiastic crowd, who turned out to greet the city's newest residents. It was said that when the train arrived, it effectively doubled the population of Venice. The paper reported that it was possibly the largest turnout of its kind ever in the history of Sarasota County.

Once all the cadets had departed the special train, they fell into formation on the station platform and then marched through town to the San Marco Building. The paper reported that "the crowd of people who walked along with the cadets, and the long line of automobiles that followed, had the resemblance of a military parade."

The ground floor of the San Marco was dedicated to classrooms while the upper two floors served as dorm rooms for the cadets. In addition to hosting the school's cafeteria, rooms in the Hotel Venice served as

KMI Cadets saying farewell to the local girls at the Venice Train Depot as they prepare for their return to Lyndon, Kentucky, circa 1950s. *Venice Historical Resources.*

Cadets in the classroom, no date. *Venice Historical Resources.*

residence for some of the faculty and administrators, as well as the younger students. The building located between the two also housed faculty, as well as KMI's infirmary.

The school wasted no time settling in. Classes were held the day after arrival. Cadets received general education courses as well as training in military science. Each cadet was assigned a military rifle that they had to clean weekly. Cadets who completed four years of study at KMI were granted the provisional rank of infantry captain in the U.S. Army upon graduation, while three-year students were able to qualify as lieutenants.

The first formal dress parade of the season was held on the afternoon of Sunday, January 15. The cadets held formation on Tampa Avenue in front of the San Marco, since preparation of the parade field (today's Centennial Park) was not yet complete. Faculty members reviewed the battalion in the parade.

It is little wonder that, along with the benefit of winters spent in Florida, the school's enrollment increased to 275 cadets in just four years. With KMI's future intact, Richmond purchased the two former hotels in 1939, along

KMI drill team on the parade grounds, 1955. *Venice Historical Resources.*

with the former Orange Blossom Garage (current Venice Theatre), which would serve as KMI's gymnasium, military science offices and classrooms and the armory where the rifles were kept.

Venice made available to the school the use of the city's bathhouse at the beach, which contained showers and dressing rooms. The school also had use of the local nine-hole golf course and clubhouse.

Tuition at KMI in 1933 amounted to $950 per year, which included the cost of meals and train travel to Venice. The Depression did not directly affect the school's enrollment, and spending the winter months in sunny Florida was certainly a marketing benefit. Advertisements promoting KMI appeared in numerous national magazines.

Through its ROTC affiliation, KMI was assigned regular army personnel to teach military science courses. They also oversaw drills, dress parades and other military exercises. The school held formal dress parades on alternate Sunday afternoons that drew thousands of onlookers, who drove from as far away as Tampa and Fort Myers to witness the pageantry.

Each day's activities were regulated by recorded bugle calls played on loudspeakers throughout the campus. Students awoke at 6:30 a.m. to the sound of reveille and retired each evening at 10:00 p.m. to the sound of taps. All cadets went through drill exercises three times each week. They also participated in athletic activities every afternoon at 3:30 p.m. following classes. The entire corps marched to meals in the mess hall, located in the former Hotel Venice dining room. During inclement weather, they held formations in the grand hallway of the San Marco.

Religious "Vespers" services were held in the school's gymnasium. In 1935, Colonel Richmond met with Monsignor Charles Elslander of Saint Martha Catholic Church in Sarasota with a request to begin holding services in the Venice area. Richmond pointed out that his Catholic students and faculty had to make a thirty-six-mile round trip to Sarasota each week to attend Mass. As a result of their meeting, the Church of the Epiphany began as a mission of the Sarasota church, with services held only during the winter months in Venice's Gulf Theatre, which was located near the intersection of Nassau Street and Venice Avenue. The altar was reportedly set up between the popcorn machine and the soft drink dispenser. About twenty people attended the first mass in the theater.

Cadets enjoyed Mondays free from class to enjoy leisurely activities. They were forbidden to ride in cars unless with family members. They were allowed, however, to maintain fishing boats, and there were no specific rules against flying in airplanes. Several cadets over the years took flying lessons at the local airports or rented airplanes, having already possessed their flying licenses. Bill Baldwin, who graduated from KMI in 1961, recalled that a

KMI track and field team with Valencia Hotel in the background, no date. *Venice Historical Resources.*

103

group of them would pool their funds on days off, and classmate Roy Sneed would rent an airplane for $100 to fly from the Venice Airport to Miami or Fort Myers for the day.

During their winter sojourn, cadets competed against local teams in various sports, including baseball, basketball, swimming and tennis. Many cadets and teams received state and regional honors over the years.

KMI's motto was "Character Makes the Man," which reflected the school's honor code. Cadets signed an oath for each test they took that stated they had neither given nor received help on their exam. Those who committed major infractions of the rules such as drinking, stealing or cheating could expect to find themselves on the next bus home.

The families of cadets who visited during the winter session would stay at nearby hotels, such as the Venezia, the El Patio and the Park View Hotel. In the 1930s, families could also rent some of the homes that had been abandoned during the Depression.

The City of Venice and KMI enjoyed a strong relationship during its thirty-seven years. During the war years, for example, some of the cadets volunteered to maintain surveillance at night on Venice's beaches for any enemy U-boats that might attempt to send spies ashore during cover of darkness.

Colonel Alex Hodgin, who graduated from KMI in 1949 and would later serve as the school's last commandant, recalled an incident in the late 1940s when Venice's mayor made a rather unusual request of the school. The city wanted the Florida Department of Transportation (FDOT) to install a traffic light at the intersection of U.S. 41 and Venice Avenue. Venice first had to prove the need for the light, however, before FDOT would consider such a request. To help validate the need, the request was made for KMI's battalion of cadets to march around the intersection a few times, thereby demonstrating the large amount of pedestrian traffic. As a result, Venice was successful in obtaining its first traffic light.

Cracks in the town-gown relationship began to appear in the spring of 1970 when the March 26 edition of the *Venice Gondolier* confirmed the rumor that KMI might not be returning to its winter home. Although no formal announcement was forthcoming, the school's director of athletics sent letters one month later to all area high schools, informing them not to put KMI on their schedules for the following year.

KMI formally closed in the spring of 1971, a victim of the increasing antiwar sentiment against the Vietnam War. Despite the school's abrupt closing, however, the relationship between KMI alumni and the community continued. Former students and their families vacationed or retired to the

Suncoast. Alumni reunions were held in Venice every four years. And in 2014, at the urging of the City of Venice, the Florida legislature renamed the north bridge onto the island of Venice in honor of KMI. Exhibits that tell the school's history are maintained both in the city's museum in the Triangle Inn and in the grand lobby of the San Marco.

THE WAR YEARS

By 1940, the American economy was escaping the lingering effects of the Great Depression. Life in Venice, however, had changed little, as there was no local industry and the population had only increased by about two hundred people during the previous decade. Perhaps the only two financial bright spots for the "town forgotten" occurred in 1933 with the opening of Dr. Fred Albee's Florida Medical Center and the Kentucky Military Institute (KMI), which brought its school and financial support to the community each winter season.

The country was still at peace in the summer of 1940, although Europe was in chaos. France had already fallen to the Nazis, and Britain had its proverbial back against the wall. Congress was against getting involved in the growing war, although President Franklin Roosevelt privately felt that the country's involvement was inevitable.

The answer to the question of involvement came on December 7, 1941, when the Japanese launched a surprise attack on American forces at Pearl Harbor and the island of Oahu. Four days later, Germany and Italy declared war on the United States. The challenge for America was in building a military force that could effectively fight three countries at once. At the time, the country's military readiness ranked nineteenth worldwide, behind countries such as Holland and Portugal. The nation was far from being a superpower.

Florida would play a strategic role in not only protecting our shores and airspace but also preparing tens of thousands of recruited civilians for

Flight line at the VAAB, 1943. *Venice Historical Resources.*

combat. The United States established more than 170 military installations, including 43 army airfields, in Florida during the war years. And one of those would be in Venice, forever changing the dynamic of the little "City on the Gulf." The Suncoast provided ideal conditions for training soldiers. In addition to its abundance of sunshine and unpopulated shoreline, there also were no barrier islands at Venice, providing direct access to the Gulf of Mexico. Years before the idea of an airbase in Venice was considered, military flight crews stationed in Sarasota conducted drills off the coast.

An article in the March 19, 1938 edition of the *Sarasota Herald* described two days of combat drills held over the Gulf waters with pursuit (fighter) planes zooming low over the city. "With a cloudless sky and perfect visibility, quite a gallery of citizens and cadets, the latter lining the roof of Kentucky Military Institute [San Marco building], were enabled to follow the air drills and observed the pursuit planes diving upon the target to loose the machine gun bursts." The article also stated the pursuit planes engaged in simulated "dog fights" to the accompaniment of "machine gun staccato" as part of their training.

On March 4, 1941, Venice realtor Finn Casperson sent a telegram to the War Department, offering three thousand acres of Gulf-front property south of the city for consideration as a possible training area for the Army Air Corps. Finn's older brother, O.W. Casperson, acquired the land in 1935. Seven days later, Casperson received a favorable response from Major General E.S. Adams. On March 12, Colonel Ralph Hill of the Army's Plans & Training Division of Coast Artillery arrived in Venice for a personal inspection of the property under consideration.

On July 16, the War Department announced that it approved the Venice site for an anti-aircraft cantonment. The headline in the *Sarasota Herald-Tribune* on that Wednesday announced, "ARMY PICKS VENICE SITE FOR PROBABLE NEW CAMP." The article went on to state that although the army had not yet completed plans for the cantonment, the extensive study "indicates a probable capacity of 30,000 men with adequate housing facilities, administration buildings, officers' clubs and a large hospital." The article further stated that under army regulations, the camp should be completed and ready for use within six months of signing the contract.

The army retained the firm of Frank Bail & Associates from Fort Myers to conduct a survey of the property. Under the supervision of the army's construction quartermaster, Lieutenant Edward Kersting, they completed the work on January 28, 1942. Plans for an anti-aircraft installation, however, never materialized. Time passed and residents began to worry that Venice might never realize those war plans. In May 1942, however, the Army Air Corps expressed a new interest in using the site as a training base for "air service groups," military units that could be sent to forward bases to establish multiple ground-based services in support of flying combat missions overseas.

These service groups consisted of army troops well trained in airplane maintenance and supply. Their purpose was to be mobile enough to follow combat organizations into battle and to handle administrative services and maintenance support to as many as eight combat squadrons simultaneously, each of which would likely be based in different locations. This would allow airborne squadrons to focus on combat missions. The training of these groups was under the leadership of the commanding general of the Air Service Command. It is important to note that during World War II, America's military air forces operated collectively as a component of the U.S. Army. This organizational structure continued until the implementation of the National Security Act of 1947.

By the end of May, representatives of the Army Air Corps and the Army Corps of Engineers had arrived on site and established an office in the El

Two servicemen doing propellor repairs, 1943. *Venice Historical Resources.*

Patio Hotel to begin detailed planning of the base. Construction materials began arriving by truck and train, and the army retained the J.B. Green Construction Company to begin construction of the water, electricity, and sewer systems. What initially began as a cantonment for about nine hundred men was soon increased to accommodate more than four thousand soldiers. The base was bounded on the north by San Marco Drive, on the east by U.S. 41, on the west by the Gulf of Mexico and on the south by Red Lake. The site would include flight line facilities and two one-mile-long hardened runways, one running east–west and the other northeast–southwest. A third runway, oriented from the southeast to the northwest, was added later for expanded flight operations. The base consisted of 1,669 acres, larger than the city of Venice itself.

The army believed that the best way to train air service groups was by locating an already established "parent" group on a small airfield where soldiers could learn through on-the-job training. Following that model, the 27th Service Group, stationed at MacDill Field in Tampa, relocated to Venice.

Main entrance to the air base, circa 1940. *Venice Historical Resources.*

The 37th Service Squadron of that group was the first to arrive in Venice on July 7, 1942. Its assignment was to provide security for the burgeoning base until other units of the group arrived. Other units of the 27th Group began arriving during July and August, at which time the base became known as the Service Group Training Center. During those early months, most of the personnel were involved with pulling stumps, cutting weeds, and preparing the base for the reception of new trainee groups.

Life for enlisted men during the earliest days of the base construction was no picnic. Quarters consisted of winterized tents where soldiers slept on canvas cots with no mattresses or pillows. A "no furlough" policy also existed, as the 27th Service Group had the responsibility of getting the base operational as quickly as possible. The Gulf beaches were within easy walking distance, however, and offered some relief from the daily tasks.

Companies assigned to other bases began arriving for service training in the fall of 1942. The quartermaster at MacDill Field provided the food rations for the base, which required a daily seventy-mile trip each way. This created challenges in preserving perishable food during the long journey.

During its initial construction phase, the base experienced one of the area's rainy seasons, proving the sewerage and drainage system inadequate. Septic tanks had been established for each of the base's latrines as well as the mess hall. The army addressed the problem by constructing a modern sewerage disposal plant, as well as improving the drainage ditches to retain the storm water runoff.

Hutments at the Venice Army Air Base, 1943. *Venice Historical Resources.*

By the end of 1942, the Service Group Training Center was prepared to adequately train other service groups. It established several schools covering a variety of pertinent subjects. Included among these specialty schools was the Air Corps Supply School, the Administration School, and the First Sergeant's School. This was in addition to regular classes in such disciplines as camouflage, aircraft identification, booby traps, field sanitation, convoys, and bivouacs. Some of the most important schools at the base were designed to teach the proper maintenance of airplane engines. One of the first focused on the Allison engines, which powered planes such as the P-39 and P-40 fighters. Other schools covered the Rolls-Royce Merlin engines, used in P-51s, and the Pratt and Whitney engines, which powered the P-47s.

One major requirement of the base was an adequate military hospital, since the closest existing facility was at MacDill Field in Tampa. After extensive surveys, the army decided that the quickest and most cost-effective solution to the challenge was to convert Dr. Fred Albee's Florida Medical Center in the former Park View Hotel for military use. This area hospital, with as many as 250 available beds, would offer a variety of medical services,

(G-715-777L)(4-16-43-2P-12")(ALLISON ENG. CLASS.A.A.B.VENICE.FLA.)

Allison aircraft engine class at Venice Army Air Base, 1943. *Venice Historical Resources.*

not only to personnel stationed in Venice but also to military installations in Sarasota and Fort Myers. The army nurses stayed at the Granada Apartments, located just two blocks from the hospital. All departments in the converted hospital were fully operational by September 1, 1943. Treating injured and ailing soldiers was its first priority, but the hospital also maintained an active OB clinic, delivering its first baby on September 7, 1943. By the end of the war, the hospital had delivered 378 babies to area military families.

Colonel Vincent B. Dixon became the new base commander in early 1943. Upon his arrival, Dixon opened a base headquarters. He improved the living conditions of the enlisted men and reinstated a system of furloughs. He also introduced new facilities at the base, including a library, theater, and a service club. A new chapel offered services for Protestant, Catholic and Jewish members. There was also a student pilot officer's club, built in the present mobile home park. Instructor pilots and other officers permanently assigned to the base leased the clubhouse at the former Venice Golf and Country Club (current site of the Publix Shopping Center on Tamami Trail) to serve as their own officer's club. The former Tower Garage on

Tampa Avenue became the base commissary. The Venice USO, with its headquarters in the Banyan House on Harbor Drive, provided dances for the soldiers in the KMI gymnasium (presently the Venice Theatre).

During this time, the designation of the base changed from being a Service Group Training Center to Venice Army Air Base. This enabled the 27th Service Group to focus its efforts on training soldiers assigned to the service groups. By October 1943, a total of nine service groups had received their training at the base. Of particular interest among the training groups was the 14th Service Group, which was made up of about four hundred Chinese American soldiers. These soldiers generated a good deal of interest locally upon their arrival on January 16, 1944. Their training focused on special situations they might encounter on their deployment to China. The soldiers trained in Venice until October 2, 1944.

Because the base lacked on-base housing for officers and married men, their families sought rented rooms or houses in Venice. Children attended local schools, and military families engaged in myriad community activities. Because gasoline was rationed, Venice residents were encouraged to offer

Chaplain John B. Hunter at the Venice Army Air Base, circa 1940. *Venice Historical Resources.*

P-47 Thunderbolt landing at VAAB, 1943. *Venice Historical Resources.*

rides to any servicemen wishing to visit Sarasota. The corner of Venice Avenue and the Tamiami Trail served as a "waiting point," marked by a wooden sign featuring a large hand "thumbing" a ride.

The base's mission expanded on June 7, 1943, with the arrival of the 13th Fighter Squadron and, shortly thereafter, the 14th Fighter Squadron of the 53rd Fighter Group from Page Field in Fort Myers. These squadrons were previously operational units deployed from Dale Mabry Airfield near Tallahassee to the Panama Canal area shortly after the Pearl Harbor attack to support defense of that strategic asset. After a year there on station, the 53rd Fighter Group was deployed to Page Field, and from there, two of the group's three squadrons were sent to Venice. The squadrons served as training units whose mission was to train combat fighter pilots and ground crewmen. Both squadrons arrived with P-39s, an older model plane, for use in training. P-47s and P-40s would eventually replace them, and they in turn were replaced by P-51 Mustangs in early 1945.

Because much of the aerial training took place over Gulf waters, the army kept crash boats on constant alert at the former BLE Realty docks located at the Venice Inlet. The crew members and their families lived in nearby cottages, so they could quickly respond to any overwater airplane incidents. Their primary mission was to rescue any flight crew members, followed by recovery of aircraft, if possible, for salvage purposes. On occasion, Venice residents reported finding pieces of aircraft washing up on Venice's beaches after plane accidents. These first responders were responsible for patrolling a forty-mile stretch of coastline, extending from Midnight Pass in the north to Old Blind Pass between Sanibel and Captiva Islands to the south. A detachment of the unit was based in Punta Gorda, responsible for operations in Charlotte Harbor as well as assisting with recovery efforts in the Gulf.

Having received their basic flight training elsewhere, the pilots undergoing combat flight training at Venice experienced 80 hours of flight time and 180 hours of classroom work over a seven- to eight-week period. At their peak in 1944, the two squadrons were producing 25 to 30 graduate pilots per month and approaching some 90,000 hours of flight time by utilizing two training shifts per day. With an emphasis on safety and under the best of conditions, flying was still a dangerous occupation. From June 1943 to October 1945, there were 151 aircraft accidents at Venice Field, averaging more than 5 per month, many of which proved fatal. Overall, 941 aircraft were lost, and more than 1,900 airmen were killed in aircraft-related accidents in Florida during the war.

On January 15, 1944, based on the expanding emphasis placed on fighter pilot training taking place at Venice, the Air Service Command transferred command of Venice Army Air Base to the Third Air Force. At any one time, the base had as many as six thousand military and civilian personnel stationed there. It is estimated that more than twenty thousand men received ground and air training in Venice during the war, many of whom went on to serve in combat theaters.

Venice received an added boost in manpower toward the end of the war when two hundred German prisoners of war were transferred to the base to perform certain tasks such as kitchen duty, motor pool and carpentry. One resident remembered seeing some prisoners clearing the beaches of debris and seaweed. Housing for the prisoners was in a special stockade with military police assigned to guard them. An article in the July 6, 1945 edition of the *Sarasota Herald-Tribune* informed readers that the prisoners were there to free up American soldiers for more important duties and to perform jobs for which civilian workers could not be found. The article

Working on a plane crash in the Gulf of Mexico, 1943. *Venice Historical Resources.*

stated, "The prisoners are paid 80 cents a day in canteen coupons, with a sharply curtailed list of items available."

Following Germany's surrender in May 1945, the military began reducing forces. However, the United States still needed troops to continue the war against Japan. For that reason, training continued at Venice Army Air Field until the United States dropped atomic bombs on Hiroshima and Nagasaki in August of that year. After Japan formally surrendered on September 2, Venice Field received orders to begin closing the base, commencing on October 1, with completion required by December 1, 1945. A "caretaker" force of about one hundred soldiers remained to secure the property. Base assets, including everything from tools to large buildings, were auctioned off to the highest bidders.

On April 7, 1946, city officials and the Venice Chamber of Commerce received letters from the War Assets Administration, advising them that the city could obtain all or part of the $3 million airbase as an outright gift from the federal government if Venice chose to move at once to protect its interests. The city responded by filing an application for a temporary use of the field before the army transferred the base on April 20 to the federal civilian department. On May 26, Venice was granted a license to operate the airport and take over the runways, three hangars, two auxiliary buildings and various maintenance equipment, even though the government still owned the property. Any net proceeds generated by the city, however, were to be applied to an "airport fund," turning the airport operation into a self-supporting enterprise. Several of the buildings on base were repurposed and relocated to city-owned property for use in Venice. One of the buildings was used as city hall, while the base chapel became the first Catholic church in town. Some of the soldiers who had been stationed at Venice Army Air Base during the war returned to spend their retirement years in the area, including the former base commander, Colonel Vincent Dixon.

AMERICA'S NEED FOR THE Venice Army Air Base concluded with the end of the Second World War. As the Cold War began, however, there was still a role for Venice to play within the Armed Forces. The military developed a new communications system called Long-Range Navigation (LORAN). It utilized a network of radio transmitter sites providing signaling to ships and planes that enabled them to fix their positions over long distances. One such station, consisting of three buildings—a supply hut, office hut and equipment building, along with two transmitting towers—was set up in 1949 by the U.S. Air Force on the beach along South Harbor Drive, just south of today's Service Club Park. After installation and testing, the air force declared the site operational in August 1951. The U.S. Coast Guard took over management of the site in February 1955, operating the site until December 1980. With the advent of satellite-based navigation technology such as the Global Positioning System (GPS), the Venice LORAN station became obsolete and was deactivated.

The air force contacted city officials during the summer of 1959 to discuss plans for support of a new Air Defense Missile System. On June 17, its contractor, Chance-Vought Aircraft Inc., signed a lease with the city for a missile launch facility on three acres of beachfront property located where the Venice Pier is today. The lease called for $1,000 per month for an initial period of four months, with six missile launches taking place during that time. The contract was subject to renewal approved by Chance-Vought and the City of Venice. The purpose of this site was to launch Chance-Vought Regulus II missiles. The U.S. Navy developed the Regulus II in the 1950s as an advanced submarine-launched cruise missile for use against land-based

LORAN transmitter at the Vencie Air Base LORAN Station, 1952. *Venice Historical Resources.*

targets. When the missiles became obsolete, the U.S. Air Force acquired them for potential target vehicles.

The Regulus missiles served as simulated targets for testing the Bomarc air defense missiles, a supersonic surface-to-air weapon capable of carrying a nuclear warhead. During one of the initial drone launches from Venice, an intercepting Bomarc made a direct hit on the Regulus target, destroying it in flight. The Regulus test flights were conducted from June 1959 through March 1961. The missiles were launched from a 17-foot ramp constructed on a concrete pad 100 by 117 feet. They were launched in the direction of Eglin Air Force Base in Florida's Panhandle, cruising to an altitude of 40,000 feet and then descending toward Eglin's Auxiliary Field No. 2. Support material for the launch site was stored in a former VAAB hangar at the west end of the field.

In November 1961, the air force negotiated another agreement with the City of Venice, this time allowing for a series of rocket firings using the Nike-Cajun missile as a vehicle for conducting high-altitude (50,000 to 100,000 feet) atmospheric research. The Nike-Cajun, a two-stage solid fuel rocket, was designed for research but was based on the Army's Nike Ajax missile system developed for surface-to-air defense. The first rocket launch occurred on December 21, 1961, with a plan for an average two launches per month

Regulus II target missiles at the Venice Air Base, circa 1960. *Venice Historical Resources.*

through August 1962. The launch site was built on the same location as was used for the Regulus missile program.

An incident occurred on Friday, March 16, 1962, when the first stage of a launch went awry and landed on a vacant lot between two houses in the 500 block of Riviera Street, about five blocks north of the airport. According to an article in the March 22 edition of the *Venice Gondolier*, no damage was reported other than the crater created with the booster that buried "all but about a few inches of its 13-foot length…and had to be removed with a winch." Venice Mayor Smyth Brohard wrote a letter to the U.S. Air Force, expressing the city's dismay over the mishap, stating that unless the military could ensure that such an incident would not be repeated, the city might ask for the launch site to be closed. No other incidents were reported, and the site closed on August 15, 1962.

THE GREATEST SHOW ON EARTH

One of the greatest events in the history of Venice occurred on the evening of December 17, 1959. Bud Wimmers, longtime promoter of the city and recently elected president of the Venice Area Chamber of Commerce, received a phone call from old friend Bill Perry, who served as publicity director for the Ringling Bros. and Barnum & Bailey Circus. "He called me and asked, 'Do you have something that will house the circus? I can't give you a yes or no, but do you have it?'"

When Wimmers assured him that land in Venice was indeed available, Perry asked if they could come and look at it that night. "So they came down and looked at [the property] with flashlights. Then, there was the proposition of meeting with the town council." Wimmers said that they could only locate one council member that evening but arranged for a closed-door meeting with circus officials on Saturday morning. "They came out of [the meeting] and said everything was fine. The deal was closed with a handshake."

The circus was leaving Sarasota because it no longer needed all two hundred acres on the city's east side that had served as its winter quarters since 1927. Having sold the property to the Arvida Corporation for about $350,000, Ringling officials gave the Sarasota County Chamber of Commerce until December 16 to recommend a suitable smaller space. When the chamber was unable to accommodate the circus's needs, Venice was selected as the best alternative with available rail connection.

Arthur Concello, executive director of the circus, announced on December 19 that a tentative agreement had been signed with the city to lease approximately fifteen acres adjacent to U.S. 41 for $1,000 per year with an option to lease an additional eighty acres should the circus proceed with plans for a proposed $1 million "Disneyland-like" tourist attraction.

Venice Mayor Smyth "Smitty" Brohard said that the lease would be for thirty years, with an option for an additional twenty years. The agreement, he added, was contingent on approval by the Federal Aviation Authority (FAA) since the property was located on the northeast corner of land previously occupied by the Venice Army Air Base.

The community, in general, was ecstatic about the newest addition. The *Venice Gondolier* ran an editorial with a headline proclaiming, "Yes, Venice, There Is a Santa Claus." After all, the siding on every circus railroad car would proclaim Venice as its headquarters and winter home. "It's the biggest thing Venice has ever had," added Wimmers.

A few residents were concerned, however, about how hosting the "Greatest Show on Earth" might adversely affect the city's quality of life. At a city council meeting in January, local realtor Finn Casperson and council member Harry H. Britton Jr. said that at least two weeks should be provided for Venetians to study the lease. Even David C. Kelley, the FAA's district engineer in Miami, questioned whether the proposed lease needed further consideration.

After numerous conferences and discussions with all interested parties, a revised contract was signed on April 29, 1960. The circus immediately began constructing a rehearsal arena that would seat five thousand spectators, as well as other structures for storage, a wardrobe/costume shop, and general offices.

The Ringling Circus was, by far, the largest and most successful circus to call Venice home. It was not, however, the first. In November 1946, the Sparks Circus negotiated a lease with the city to use three buildings at the former Army Air Base, along with adjacent open grounds that would later be occupied by the Ringling's Circus Arena. After spending the winter months in its new home, Sparks planned a farewell benefit for residents before heading out on the road. Heavy rains canceled the performance, however, which would serve as a harbinger of what was to come. Bad weather and other challenges during the performing season ended the circus' operations. The Sparks Circus never returned to Venice.

The city would serve as the fourth location for the Ringling Circus. The five Ringling brothers, aged sixteen to thirty, originally called Baraboo, Wisconsin home, and it was there, in 1882, that they formed a song-and-dance troupe called the "Ringling Brothers Classic and Comic Opera

Constructing the Circus Arena, circa 1960. *Venice Historical Resources.*

Company." The town remained their base of operation until 1918, when the brothers purchased the Barnum & Bailey Circus and moved operations to Bridgeport, Connecticut, where the merged circuses became known as "Ringling Bros. and Barnum & Bailey Combined Shows."

In 1927, John Ringling, the last surviving brother, moved the circus closer to the $1.5 million mansion he had completed on Sarasota Bay the previous year, the Cà d'Zan. Sarasota would remain the circus's winter base for thirty-two years until streamlining the show's operations and leasing many of its animals to zoos on the East Coast facilitated the move to the smaller Venice property.

When John Ringling died on December 2, 1936, his nephew, John Ringling North, assumed control of the circus. It was during his leadership that the circus moved to its new Venice winter quarters.

By the late fall of 1960, the fifty-five-thousand-square-foot arena was nearly completed in preparation for the circus's arrival. Nearly four stories in height, the arena included two sixty-foot wings with space for staging and wardrobe. The seating was designed so that it could be lifted out of the way for rehearsals and trade show events.

Moving day occurred on the morning of November 29 as the fifteen streamlined circus cars arrived at the Venice Train Depot shortly before 9:00 a.m. An estimated ten thousand people showed up to welcome the

Aerial view of the circus arena near the airport, circa 1967. *Venice Historical Resources.*

performers to their new home. Many local businesses closed for the day, and classes were suspended so youngsters could witness the spectacle. City leaders were on hand to give speeches, "while the Venice High School band played and drum majorettes cavorted on the station platform," reported the December 1 edition of the *Venice Gondolier*. Mayor Brohard, atop a Venice fire truck, would lead the parade of animals and performers down U.S. 41 to their new winter quarters.

"It was the greatest welcome ever afforded any organization in the history of the city," added *Banner Line*, a circus publication of the time.

By the mid-twentieth century, American tastes were beginning to change, and what the circus needed was a P.T. Barnum–type promoter who could provide fresh ideas to a nearly century-old entertainment venue. That person surfaced in 1956 in the form of Irvin Feld, a promoter who operated a chain of record stores in Washington, D.C. He suggested to North that he take his circus out of the canvas "Big Tops" and move them into the large arenas found in major American cities. North took Feld's advice, and the last "Greatest Show on Earth" appeared under canvas on July 16, 1956, in

Circus parade from the train depot to its winter headquarters, 1960. *Venice Historical Resources.*

Pittsburgh, Pennsylvania. He also hired Feld to help promote the circus. "For 11 years, I did everything for the circus—bookings, promotion. Everything except produce the show. It became an obsession with me," Feld told a reporter in 1978.

In 1967, Feld and his brother, Israel, joined with former Houston Astros baseball team owner Ray Hofienz to purchase the circus. After Hofienz suffered a stroke, the toy company Mattel Inc. purchased the circus in February 1971, with Feld staying on to manage it. Feld and his son, Kenneth Feld, repurchased the circus in 1982. The family continues to own the circus and other entertainment properties. Following Irvin's death in 1984, Kenneth was named chairman and CEO of Feld Entertainment.

In all, the circus would spend only about six weeks in Florida, the rest of the time performing in dozens of cities throughout the United States and Canada. The circus generally would arrive in Venice during the first part of December, at which time employees would enjoy the holidays relaxing with their families. Two weeks of rehearsals for new acts would then begin early in January before heading out on the road for the touring season. Shows were only held in the arena on weekends, although visitors could wander the grounds throughout the week. The first preview performance was held in the completed arena in early 1962. Sigrid Gebel, a performer with horses and the widow of fellow performer and legendary animal trainer Gunther Gebel-Williams, said that people would line up in lawn chairs around the arena to purchase tickets. And most shows sold out.

"He [Gunther] loved the audiences here," she said. "They stood in line when he did outside practices in the cage. No matter if he had a toothache or his tummy felt lousy, he would put on a show, whether it was for 200 people or 20,000 in the [Madison Square] Garden."

Six months after he became president and producer of the circus, Irvin Feld announced the creation of a second touring unit, to be known as the Red Unit, beginning with the 1969 season. The original unit was called the Blue Unit. With one unit traveling forty-seven weeks a year, scores of cities in the United States and Canada would still miss the opportunity of experiencing the circus. Adding the Red Unit meant that most Americans could now see the Greatest Show on Earth. The Red Unit would debut in

Gunther Gebel-Williams rehearsing with a tiger, circa 1970. *Venice Historical Resources.*

126

odd years, while the Blue Unit would debut in even years. Gunther Gebel-Williams was the star of the Red Unit, while another famous animal trainer, Charlie Baumann, headlined the Blue Unit.

In a December 22, 1983 interview with the *Venice Gondolier*, Kenneth Feld said that "each unit had about 350 employees, with a combined total of 83 railroad cars and more than 500 animals." The circus trains, each extending more than a mile in length, would travel more than thirty thousand miles across America and Canada each season—the largest privately owned train in the world.

The circus never owned locomotives; those remained the property of the various rail lines. Seaboard Airline Railroad locomotives, for example, would bring the trains to Venice and return when it was time to leave for the new season. Each train car was at least seventy feet in length and varied from flat cars and stock cars that transported the animals to more than thirty passenger cars for the performers, circus personnel and their families. The stock cars, carrying the elephants and other animals, would be coupled directly behind the locomotive for the smoothest possible ride. It normally took about six hours to unload the train and twelve hours to set up for a show.

The performers' cars were assigned based on one's status in the show and were outfitted according to the occupant's tastes. One of the larger units, for example, might contain a standard living room, kitchen, bathroom and bedrooms. Each car contained its own generator for producing heat, light, and air conditioning.

Tragedy struck in 1962 when a brush fire caused by a stray spark from an acetylene torch destroyed fifteen circus wagons and a "Big Top," which had been used in the "old circus days." The fire occurred on a siding located about a half mile east of the winter quarters. Ownership of the destroyed equipment had been transferred to Circus Enterprises some time before for a proposed circus museum. According to an article in the March 22, 1962 issue of the *Venice Gondolier*, several area fire departments, aided by circus workers, battled the fire for nearly three hours before it was brought under control. Workers pulled some of the more valuable circus wagons away from the burning brush so they could be repaired. William Perry, now head of Circus Enterprises, said that the best of the parade wagons, coaches and carriages and many of the floats from recent circus spectaculars had been stored in an old airport hangar building and were not damaged.

From September 1963 until April 1964, a total of thirty episodes of a television program called *The Greatest Show on Earth* appeared on the ABC television network and included many famous guest stars. Produced by

The Gaona Family Trapeze Act, 1965. *Venice Historical Resources.*

Desilu Studios, with much of the taping done on location in Venice, Jack Palance starred as the circus boss and Tuesday Weld as an aerialist with the show. The program, of course, was based on the 1952 movie of the same name, which was filmed at the circus's Sarasota location.

The "Flying Gaonas"—comprising brothers Armondo, Ricardo, Tito and sister Chela—were already internationally famous with the Clyde Beatty Cole Bros. Circus, as well as other companies throughout Europe, when a Ringling agent saw their act in Sweden. They signed a contract with the circus in 1965 but were allowed to finish their European commitments before joining the circus on the road in Raleigh, North Carolina, on February 15, 1966. Ironically, the Gaonas already lived in Venice, less than a mile from the circus's winter quarters. They would remain one of the most famous acts with Ringling for the next nineteen years. When asked how the Ringling circus compared to other circus companies they had worked with, Tito replied with a smile that it was simply "the Greatest Show on Earth": "For you, as a performer, you had to be with the best acts to be with Ringling." Having performed his first triple somersault on the trapeze by age twelve, Tito would go on to set the record for consecutive triple somersaults, performing it nearly seven hundred times per season.

Master clown Lou Jacobs teaching students at Clown College, circa 1968. *Venice Historical Resources.*

By the mid-1960s, the number of clowns in the circus had dwindled to little more than a handful. Many of them had been with the circus for a quarter century or more and were reaching retirement age. Irvin Feld not only needed to increase their number, but he also wanted to generate new energy in this select group of performers. To remedy the problem, he created what would become known as the Clown College in the fall of 1967.

Charles "Chuck" Sidlow had never been to a circus when he auditioned for the college in Philadelphia at age seventeen and became a member of the class of 1977. Known in greasepaint as "Chucko," Sidlow would go on to become the youngest boss clown in the history of the circus. The Clown College would hold auditions in major American cities, usually at the beginning of the week, to help generate publicity for the circus show later in the week, he said. "During its heyday, the college would receive as many as 5,000 applications per season, of which 50 would be accepted. The circus would then only hire 8 to 10 graduates. They would be offered a one-year contract with the circus, followed by a two-year apprenticeship."

Clown College offered free tuition, but students had to provide their own room and board. The program lasted about eight weeks, Sidlow said, and usually began in early September. Students rented rooms at the Venice Villas motel on Venice Avenue and either ate on their own or at a small restaurant in the arena called the Pie Car. "Those kids, mostly in their late teens, worked from six or seven in the morning to all night long. But they were in town, spending money, and experiencing the city. A lot of them who weren't offered a contract stayed in Venice, or would return to Venice, because Venice was such a unique part of their life. It changed so many lives of the people who went to that college, it became part of their being."

College students were responsible not only for developing their clown characters but also for making their own costumes, makeup and props. There were twenty-eight clowns assigned to each circus unit, three of them women. They would perform about twenty minutes of warm-up routines before the main show began. The show itself, which lasted about three hours, had five major acts, while the clowns had fifteen different routines, providing entertainment between the acts, Sidlow said. The clowns also had to be prepared to improvise and provide a distraction should any emergency or unplanned event occur during a show.

The show itself was a breeze, Sidlow said, compared to getting ready and cleaning up afterward. "The consistency of quality and family values and presentations never ceased. With 150 performers, 250 animals, 18 shows a week, 48 weeks a year, it was not only entertaining. I think we made the public feel like they were part of something very special, not just there to watch."

There never were any days off when the circus was touring. The children of performers, many of whom were given their own acts in the show, continued their studies with a tutor in a stateroom on the train. The Greatest Show on Earth was indeed a village on wheels.

Although the circus was made up of performers from many different countries, the children never experienced a language barrier, said Sidlow. "They spoke their own language to each other and they played together all the time. These families were so proud to be in America and to show people what they could do, where they came from with their national music and their wardrobes. You could walk through the train cars and it was like a United Nations of food, music, excitement, and culture. They never let their guard down, but they never forgot they were in America. Many of them ended up homesteading here in Sarasota County."

The April 17, 1993 edition of the *Venice Gondolier* announced that the Clown College was moving from its Venice home of twenty-three years to the Ringling's original site in Baraboo, Wisconsin. After three years there, however, the college moved yet again, this time to the Sarasota Opera House just twenty miles up the road from its original location. The college continued to operate there until 1997, when Ringling's Clown College finally closed its doors for good. The needs of the circus were changing, and during its three decades of existence, nearly 1,500 clowns had graduated. The college had more than served its purpose.

The Ringling Bros. and Barnum & Bailey Circus celebrated its centennial year in 1984, tracing its roots back to the brothers' humble beginnings in Wisconsin. While a cause for celebration, the relationship between the circus and the City of Venice was also beginning to strain. According to a December 17, 1984 article in the *Venice Gondolier*, Kenneth Feld said that the friction with the city began several years before when Venice's fire marshal ordered the circus to remove one thousand seats from the arena for safety purposes. Feld said the sixteen-thousand-seat reduction (one thousand times the sixteen shows the circus staged annually in Venice) carried an average seat price of $8, which amounted to an annual revenue loss of $128,000.

Another source of friction, Feld said, was the increasing amount the circus was being charged above its annual $20,000 assessment for off-duty police and firefighter support. And with consumer price index increases on their lease, the circus was now paying $5,500 per year for use of the fifteen-acre site. "I want to clear the air that it's my intention and the circus' intention to stay in Venice," he told city officials at a meeting in January 1985. "I want to stay in Venice. There are certain things that would make it a lot easier." To emphasize the value the circus provided Venice, the entire payroll was once distributed in $2 bills. It was a publicity stunt that captured the attention of not only local businesses but also the community at large.

A coupon survey conducted by the *Venice Gondolier* revealed that more than two thousand readers wanted the circus to remain in Venice, while fewer than fifty indicated that they would be glad to see it go. Irvin Feld promised to read each and every comment provided on the coupons.

While the Felds talked of the circus's desire to remain in Venice, officials in the City of Lakeland initiated a full-court press to persuade the show to relocate to Polk County. Fort Myers also expressed an interest in hosting the circus. Like Venice, both cities offered easily accessible rail service. Irvin Feld confirmed that the move was a possibility in the May 23, 1984 edition of the *Venice Gondolier*. He added that once a decision would be made about relocation, the show could be "out of Venice in three to four months."

Despite the threats and the competition between cities for the circus's attention, Venice remained the home of the Greatest Show on Earth. Even bigger problems were forming on the horizon, however. The Seminole Gulf Railway, based in Fort Myers, acquired the rail lines of the Seaboard Coast Line Railroad in 1987. The railway continued to serve the needs of the circus for the next five years before announcing in April 1992 that the thirteen miles of track was up for sale due to the "bleak revenue picture" of serving the Venice community going forward.

Gordon Fay, president of the railroad, told city and county officials that the deteriorating rail beds would require between $3 million and $5 million in repairs to bring the track up to viable commercial standards. To upgrade the track enough to permit the circus train to return to Venice in late 1992 would cost as much as $100,000, he added.

Sarasota County Commissioner Bob Anderson, who attended the meeting with circus officials, said that they "painted a bleak picture on revenues for continuing to serve Venice." The circus, he said, was the railroad's primary customer for the rail line, and it paid only about $10,000 per year to come into Venice for rehearsals and for quartering the two circus units.

Charles Lynch, vice-president of engineering for Seminole Gulf Railway, said that the main problem was that the railroad ties had deteriorated to the point that they could no longer support the rails. Every mile of railroad included 3,200 ties, he said, which could be replaced at the rate of 400 to 500 per day. The ballast, or gravel and dirt that supported the ties, would also have to be put down, graded and smoothed.

In an article published in the April 13, 1992 edition of the *Sarasota Herald-Tribune*, circus spokeswoman Susannah Smith said, "Right now we are a train without a home. I can't tell you how many people here are sick at heart, thinking about not being in Venice." The article went on to point out that former circus performers settled in Venice, current staff members lived there and the company employed eighty-two Sarasota County residents. Circus officials described the tracks as their lifeline since the show traveled by rail wherever it went.

Other Florida cities expressed an interest in hosting the circus if the rail problem could not be resolved. Lakeland, for example, reminded officials that they had a civic center where performers could rehearse. Even Punta Gorda Mayor Rufus Lazzell called in to put his city's name on the relocation possibility list.

"Can we maintain our home?" Smith asked rhetorically. "Venice is home for Ringling Bros. and Barnum & Bailey Circus. And everybody wants to go home."

A task force led by the Venice Chamber of Commerce attempted to raise funds to sufficiently repair the tracks. The circus agreed to give $50,000 toward the effort, half of that in increased payments for the land leased for its winter quarters. Sarasota County pledged $75,000, and the combined amounts were used to obtain a $125,000 matching grant from the Florida Department of Transportation. In the end, the cost of maintaining the thirteen miles of track could not be justified by the small amount of revenue primarily generated by the circus. The trains relocated to the Florida State Fairgrounds in Tampa at the end of the 1992 season. Now operating as part of Feld Entertainment, the circus operations eventually relocated to Palmetto, while the company headquarters was based in Vienna, Virginia. All Feld businesses moved to a former General Electric plant in Ellenton, Florida, in 2013.

Faced with escalating production costs, the retirement of elephants from the show as a result of unsubstantiated animal mistreatment charges and declining ticket sales, the Greatest Show on Earth closed down in 2017. Feld Entertainment relaunched a version of the circus without animal performances in October 2023.

Meanwhile, what had served for more than a half century as the circus's winter quarters fell into disrepair. Volunteers led efforts to turn the former arena into a venue for various civic events, but the city's engineer eventually determined the building to be unsafe and a health hazard. Lacking funds to complete the restoration, the buildings were demolished in 2014. One building at the northern edge of the property, which was used to shelter the elephants, would later serve as home for the Italian American Club of Venice.

Demolition of Circus Arena, 2014. *Venice Historical Resources.*

Sarasota County purchased the Venice Train Depot in 1999 to be used as a bus transfer station. A $2.3 million renovation of the building was completed in 2003 and was classified that year as a county park. Two years later, it was dedicated as a railroad park in honor of volunteer Rollins W. Coakley. And on December 5, 2005, a statue of famed animal trainer Gunther Gebel-Williams was dedicated in the park.

A Seaboard red caboose was donated by CSX Transportation and placed in the park on October 16, 2003. And on February 23, 2023, a former circus train car, containing circus memorabilia, was dedicated. Serving as a museum that tells the history of the Ringling circus in Venice, the dedication was attended by Kenneth Feld, as well as many former circus performers. Both train cars and an exhibit of Venice history located in the former depot are available for touring by docent volunteers.

Venice always had a special place in the hearts of all who were associated with the circus, said Tito Gaona. "It was always very special coming home at the end of the season. It was special walking the elephants over the Circus Bridge to our winter home." Gaona added that the circus was really the sum total of the performers who were the best in their specialty. "The Gaonas, the Gunther Gebel-Williams, the Wallendas, Emmett Kelly and other circus clowns. Ringling became the Greatest Show on Earth because they were the greatest acts on Earth."

VENICE ON THE WATER

Venice enjoys the distinction of being the only city on the Suncoast that enjoys direct access to the Gulf of Mexico. It is no wonder the city's newspaper in 1927, the *Venice News*, carried the slogan: "It's a privilege to live in Florida and a distinction to live in Venice."

With its high banks and availability to open water, it was a popular hunting and fishing location for Native American tribes populating the area. And when homesteaders began moving to the area following the Civil War, they, too, were attracted to the bays teeming with fish, as well as a faster and easier way of traveling to Sarasota and other cities along Florida's southwest coast.

Early promoters of the area—like Bertha Honoré Palmer, Joseph Lord and Dr. Fred Albee—realized that Venice's waterways needed to be improved if the Suncoast was to thrive. Until about 1910, there was no direct local access to the Gulf of Mexico from these waterways. Residents had to navigate their boats about fifteen miles north to Little Sarasota Pass to reach open water.

At about the same time, an article in the *Sarasota Times* mentioned that residents living nearby noticed that heavy rains had raised the water level in Roberts Bay considerably higher than in the Gulf. Wishing to seize on the opportunity, B.F. Blackburn led an attempt to dredge an opening to the Gulf at Venice. He and about eleven other residents gathered for a picnic near what would become Casey's Pass. They brought with them drag lines and various tools to remove the sand that separated the two bodies of water. By the end of the day, they had succeeded in their task of removing enough sand and silt, thereby allowing the excess water that had accumulated in the bays to empty into the Gulf. A new passage for Venice was created. Shifting sands due to currents and storms, however, required them to repeat the procedure on multiple occasions.

Early businessmen encouraged the government to improve the waterways by widening and deepening them between Sarasota and Venice while also extending passage to the Miakka River, thereby creating a continuous inland channel into the upper end of Charlotte Harbor. In a letter to the U.S. Corps of Engineers, H.R. Dreggors of the Punta Gorda Fish Company supported the idea, saying that such an endeavor would eliminate the need for "a long run through rough and dangerous water." Added Sarasota businessman Owen Burns, "I would not favor spending Government funds on mere neighborhood joyriding projects. But this proposed canal is an integral part of a great waterway system to unite the North Atlantic seaboard with the Gulf. In importance it is to be ranked with the Mississippi and Ohio River systems."

A letter dated July 30, 1917, from the War Department to Congress contained the results of a preliminary examination of the waterways under consideration. In summary, the report stated that while improving and extending the waterways would likely benefit some tourist and pleasure travel, it would provide little support for commercial navigation. The Corps of Engineers recommended that the project "was not worthy of being undertaken by the United States."

The October 13, 1925 edition of the *Sarasota Times* reported Albee as saying that further dredging of Casey's Pass would begin shortly. "This, with the deep waters of the four bays at Venice-Nokomis will provide a harbor equal to, if not better than, any in Florida, one capable of accommodating ocean going steamers." Albee and the BLE Realty Corporation, which was negotiating to buy the Venice property from him at the time, were under the illusion that the inland waterways around Venice were deeper than they were.

The following month, the Sarasota paper announced, "Venice expects to go under the wire ahead of Sarasota in the race for deep water navigation and the bid for a port of entry." If nothing else, Albee and the BLE Realty Corporation excelled at public relations. The article went on to state that a dredge had been purchased for $65,000 "for the sole purpose of dredging a deep-water channel from the Gulf of Mexico to Casey's Pass and a land-locked harbor there, so that coastwise ships may enter with their cargoes."

A mention in the November 18, 1925 edition of the *Sarasota Times* stated that the dredge was detained in Boca Grande due to high seas. A headline

Casey's Pass, circa 1926. *Venice Historical Resources.*

in the December 3, 1925 edition of *This Week in Sarasota* announced, "Deep-water Channel to Gulf with 22 Feet of Water through the Pass at Venice May be Opened Within Next 20 Days."

A few days following the announcement, at a dinner at Villa Nokomis, Albee told attendees, "Few people realize the great importance of a deep water and land-locked harbor in the development of this rising young city of South Sarasota County." Pointing out that BLE Realty was covering the cost of the project, he added, "When the operation is completed, the BLE and the Albee interests will jointly have Casey's Pass jettied so that the sand taken out by dredging will be prevented from filling in the Pass again." He said that a survey of the seafloor determined that clay was located just a few feet below the sand layer so that jetties could be built there on a firm foundation and that it would only be necessary to dredge about six hundred feet out into the Gulf to reach thirty feet of water.

The April 20, 1926 edition of the *Sarasota Times* announced that noted harbor expert and retired Army Major General W.M. Black had been hired by BLE Realty as consultant to oversee the Venice Harbor project. The article added that Black had previously directed construction of the jetties at the mouth of the St. Johns River in Jacksonville, as well as the channel into the Port of Tampa. No record of Black's recommendations was apparently ever made public. BLE Realty did, however, retain the consulting services of his Washington, D.C.–based company, Black, McKinney & Stewart, after the contract with Southern Construction Engineers of Sarasota was terminated. Once the Brotherhood of Locomotive Engineers abandoned the Venice project, all work on Casey's Pass ceased and would not resume for a decade.

As part of New Deal legislation, Congress authorized the U.S. Army Corps of Engineers in 1934 to study the feasibility of creating an inland waterway along the Gulf Coast. Appearing before the army's Rivers and Harbors Board in Washington, D.C., U.S. Senator Royal S. Copeland (D-NY), a seasonal resident of Venice, argued the need for improvements to the area's waterways to stimulate trade and commerce. "But Florida is more than a state where trade and commerce are carried on," he is thought to have said, according to the March 26, 1935 edition of the *Sarasota Herald*. "It is a great playground, and we should contribute to the building of such playground in the interest of health."

The River and Harbor Act also authorized construction of the jetties to begin in July 1936 with an estimated cost of $65,000. Each of the jetties would be about six hundred feet long with the canal between them about eight

Final dredging of the Venice jetties, 1937. *Venice Historical Resources.*

feet deep and one hundred feet wide. Actual construction of the jetties and dredging the channel, however, did not begin until February 1937, thereby escalating the cost to $175,000. Each of the Venice jetties would consist of nineteen steel sheet cylinders, filled with rip rap and creosoted wood sheet pile bulkheads connecting the jetties to the shore. Jetty construction was completed in July 1937, and dredging of the channel was completed on October 18, 1937.

The Corps of Engineers completed its study in 1939 and recommended construction of the Intracoastal Waterway (ICW) from the Caloosahatchee River in Lee County north to the Anclote River channel in upper Pinellas County. Because of the war, however, work on several projects, including the waterway, was suspended.

In 1945, following the end of the war, and as the Venice Army Air Base was being decommissioned, Congress approved construction of the waterway. The project called for constructing a channel one hundred feet wide and nine feet deep. The need for rights-of-way and spoil areas existed all along the 152-mile route. And because the project would pass through six counties—Hillsborough, Pinellas, Manatee, Sarasota, Charlotte and Lee—a regional government entity was needed to address the myriad local challenges before a federal construction appropriation could be expected.

The Florida legislature answered the need in 1947 when it created the West Coast Inland Navigation District (WCIND), which operates under a governing board comprised of county commissioners representing each of the six counties in the special district. Counties in the district were subject to ad valorem taxes to assist in paying for construction of the waterway.

Once the WCIND board was created, the local conversation then shifted to what route the ICW would take, particularly around Venice. When the Corps made its original recommendation in 1939, it suggested paralleling the Venice shoreline, about five hundred feet east of the Gulf, and extending the channel from Roberts Bay to Lemon Bay to the south. That route might have made sense in the mid-1930s, when the proposed route was still largely undeveloped. By the late 1940s, however, development had progressed, and the shoreline route was no longer feasible.

There was a good deal of controversy over several proposed routes. Some residents opposed the entire project, stating that an inland waterway was a waste of taxpayer money. Others feared that a waterway constructed through "the middle of Venice," thereby creating a man-made island, would destroy the city. The Venice City Council suggested returning to Nolen's original idea of connecting the waterway to the Myakka River, but engineers quickly dismissed that suggestion, adding that they were not interested in opening up the "back country." City officials also suggested the waterway divert into the Gulf and bypass Venice, but that idea also was dismissed. Amid threats of lawsuits, Venice was becoming the stumbling block that might derail the entire project.

Finally, in 1951, the WCIND recommended a "C-1" route that was approved by the Corps three years later. The C-1 or "Seaboard route" would cross U.S. 41 at Hatchett Creek, extend south parallel to the railroad tracks, past the School Board and airport property and eventually connect with Lemon Bay. Although the agreed-on route would cost nearly $1.4 million more than the original route, all parties agreed on the compromise.

As part of the agreement, Venice would not be required to pay for the bridges or the relocation of utilities. It also was agreed to construct a four-lane bypass around Venice and east of the waterway. U.S. 41 would remain where it was on the city's newly created island.

Even though the Corps had yet to approve the proposed route, WCIND began acquiring necessary land and spoil areas in the waterway's path while working with numerous local agencies to resolve issues affecting its construction. Congress approved the C-1 route in 1954. It had been nearly two decades since the first survey was completed, and many residents still questioned whether the "ditch," as many called it, would ever be completed. A banner headline in the April 15, 1963 edition of the *Gondolier* announced, "Land Transfer Ends Long Canal Hassle." It became clear that the decades-long dream of an inland waterway was about to become reality.

Construction of the waterway began in Charlotte County in 1960 and at the north end of the project the following year. Dredging of the final section of waterway around Venice began in April 1965 and was completed in January 1967. In total, more than 14 million cubic yards of spoil was dredged to create the waterway around the city.

Three bascule-type bridges were constructed, connecting the mainland with the man-made island: the Hatchett Creek (KMI) Bridge to the north, the Center Road (Circus) Bridge to the south and the Venice Avenue Bridge, which was constructed over dry land. The State Road Department (today's Florida Department of Transportation) funded the north and south bridges for a combined cost of $1.3 million, and WCIND funded the Venice Avenue Bridge for $1.25 million. The State Road Department also funded construction of the U.S. 41 bypass at a cost of more than $1 million.

A formal dedication of the completed waterway was held locally on February 25, 1967. The ceremony was held at the east end of the Venice

Top: Building one of the Intracoastal Bridges, circa 1960. *Venice Historical Resources.*

Bottom: Dredge used to dig the Intracoastal Waterway, circa 1960. *Venice Historical Resources.*

Airport runway, with parking provided in the adjacent parking lot for the Ringling Circus Arena. Former Florida Governor and U.S. Senator Spessard L. Holland officiated at the ceremony, which was followed by a fish fry and fireworks.

The first annual Inland Waterway celebration was held in Venice just three months later. Festivities included both land and boat parades, an airshow, a surfing contest, and a beach concert. The Venice Avenue Bridge was formally named in honor of Colonel George Kumpe. The retired army colonel served as executive director of WCIND from 1959 until his untimely death, along with his wife, in a car accident in 1966. At the dedication ceremony, a ribbon was strung beneath the bridge, which was severed by an explosive charge.

The ICW today provides 162 miles of navigable channels, with the U.S. Coast Guard responsible for marine navigational markings and the Corps of Engineers maintaining safe passage. WCIND also continues in its role of providing regional operational responsibility for four of the affected counties (Pinellas and Hillsborough Counties have since assumed responsibility for their own portions of the waterway).

THE POSTWAR LAND BOOM YEARS

With America once again at peace, the 1950s entered a decade of optimism measured by unbridled growth and prosperity. The Suncoast also felt that resurgence. During the decade, Venice's population witnessed a surge of more than 2,700 new residents, a 373.7 percent increase over the ten-year span. Many of those new residents, seeking their place in the sun, demanded larger and more modern homes to accommodate their growing families. That demand would be met in January 1953, not only benefiting the city of Venice but also spurring development all along Florida's southwest coast.

Two brothers from New Jersey, Warren and Arthur Smadbeck, came looking for land to develop. When they told Venice realtor H.N. "Bud" Wimmers that they were looking for about eighty acres to purchase, he suggested they think on a larger scale. He told them, "What I have in mind is the South Venice area where there is about 1,800 acres. It runs from the Gulf of Mexico back to the (U.S. 41) highway. It's a beautiful piece of land."

At the Venice Chamber of Commerce's annual banquet in early January 1953, President Quentin R. Burke announced that the W&A Construction Corporation had purchased some three thousand acres of land to be developed as the South Venice Subdivision. He also announced that the chamber would be sponsoring the development to "aid local growth."

An article in the January 8, 1953 edition of the *Venice Gondolier* said that the news announced at the chamber dinner "had the effect of a bombshell" on the 174 people in attendance. Burke said the Robins Advertising Agency of

From left to right: Mayor George Youngberg Sr., Morton Robbins and Chamber of Commerce President Quentin R. Burke at banquet celebrating beginning of lot sales in South Venice, 1953. *Venice Historical Resources.*

Sarasota had been retained to launch a nationwide promotional campaign that would spend nearly $1 million on advertising. The campaign, which would be funded by the company, had already ordered $9,360 in road signs with $4,000 in print advertising budgeted for the first week. Ads would appear in most major cities east of the Mississippi River.

Located four miles south of Venice, W&A Construction Corporation plotted a total of 19,587 lots in the development. Each lot could be purchased for $200 by putting $25 down with a monthly payment of $5. "We sold the lots in two, three, and five multiples," said Wimmers in an interview. "In other words, you couldn't build a house on less than two lots because each lot was 40 by 100 feet. But wherever you sold a two-lot customer, salesmen were encouraged to sell a three-lot customer next to him. Corner lots were five lots. So, if you go and take a trip through South Venice, you're going to be amazed at the space it conveys. The only place they didn't follow that rule was on Lemon Bay Drive, which overlooked the Bay. There you could build on two lots provided you built within 18 months. That's the only place you can find houses built on two lots side by side."

The purpose of the national ad campaign was to sell the lots as quickly as possible. Most everyone was surprised, however, by the immediate response. An article in the January 15 edition of the *Gondolier* reported that 164 lots had already been sold during the three days following the initial announcement. About 500 lots were sold the following week. M.M. Robins, whose Sarasota ad agency managed the promotional campaign, said that "the exact number of sales was not known because the demand had been so great, we haven't been able to get our records together." To avoid speculators, no customer could purchase more than five lots in the subdivision.

"When I tell you people were lined up in automobiles, and came by plane and boat, I'm not lying to you," Wimmers said. "I was down there one afternoon from two o'clock until about 6:30 and I made myself $2,500. No one expected what happened when the lots went on the market."

Since roads through the development had not yet been built and, at best, consisted of little more than sandy paths through the scrub, salesmen would simply point out lots on a large plat map on the sales office wall. And for those who did not come to Venice to personally inspect the development, they

South Venice community at Lemon Bay Drive, circa 1950. *Venice Historical Resources.*

simply mailed in checks to secure a lot. Building the infrastructure became a community effort. Several local high school boys, members of a hot rod club called the Vagabonds, moonlighted before and after class driving dump trucks filled with fill to the development. And W&A Construction workers labored around the clock for nearly two years to build some ninety-five miles of road through the project.

Although many people purchased lots on speculation, houses did start appearing by the end of 1953. In the February 11, 1954 edition of the *Gondolier*, Robins announced that only about four thousand lots remained to be sold and that the national ad campaign might end within the next sixty days. He added that the sales total for the project thus far had reached about $3 million.

About 150 homes had been constructed in South Venice by 1955. Most of the homes consisted of two bedrooms and one bathroom, ranging in cost from $5,000 to $11,000. While South Venice was developing rapidly, it still lacked essential services such as phone service, local fire and police protection, and paved roads. The post office delivered mail from Tampa

Aerial view of layout of South Venice, circa 1950. *Venice Historical Resources.*

South Venice footbridge that crossed Lemon Bay, circa 1950. *Venice Historical Resources.*

each day and deposited it at a nearby motel on U.S. 41 where residents could go to retrieve it.

Seeking better representation, a small group of residents in January 1956 formed the South Venice Civic Association (SVCA). Within a year, Sarasota County designated the unincorporated area a Road District, and residents approved a special tax to repair their roads. The Smadbeck brothers also donated 1,600 feet of beachfront property as well as bridges over Lemon Bay that connected the subdivision to Manasota Key.

When the U.S. Army Corps of Engineers completed the Intracoastal Waterway in the Venice area in 1967, the footbridge connecting the subdivision to the beach property had to be removed. To provide access to the beach, the Corps of Engineers allocated $150,000 to the SVCA toward the purchase of a ferry and boat dock to transport residents across the Intracoastal Waterway. South Venice celebrated the christening of *Miss Venice*, their new ferry boat, on December 11, 1967. By the 1990s, there were more than eight thousand residents of South Venice, making it the largest subdivision in Sarasota County.

While South Venice undoubtedly had the largest impact on the city's growth, development was underway in other areas near Venice. Urban planner John Nolen's original design of Venice called for continued development south of the city along Harbor Drive and the Gulf of Mexico. When BLE Realty abandoned the Venice Project, however, those plans were shelved. The land remained untouched until the mid-1930s, when the Caspersen brothers entered the scene. Olaus and Finn Caspersen came to America from Norway with their mother at age seven. Unfamiliar with the culture and unable to speak English upon their arrival, the brothers managed to become successful businessmen. In 1936, Olaus purchased 3,600 acres of the land. He asked Finn to manage the property for him.

In 1942, Finn Caspersen sold 1,230 acres of land to the War Department for development of the Venice Army Air Base; an additional 458 acres were also leased. The land was bordered by San Marco Drive to the north, U.S. 41 to the east, Red Lake to the south and the Gulf of Mexico to the west. The base was decommissioned in 1945 and subsequently made available to the city for use as a municipal airport.

Although still considered county property, the Caspersens began to plat and sell more of their land. Gulf Shores 1 was platted on March 10, 1953, and was soon followed by Plats 2, 3 and 4. Some of these lots were slowly annexed by the City of Venice. There was concern by some homeowners, however, that further expansion might lead to rezoning and the creation of high-rise condominiums along the beach.

Gulf Shores was still undeveloped county property in 1960 and serviced by the Sheriff's Office and the Nokomis Volunteer Fire Department. In 1947, Caspersen convinced a developer named Joseph Spadaro to purchase some of their property at the south end of Harbor Drive. The self-made millionaire purchased 196 acres of land on December 19, what eventually would become known as the Golden Beach subdivision.

Born on the island of Sicily in 1883, Spadaro reportedly worked the docks in Naples before moving to New York City in 1900 and going to work for the city's street department. He started his own construction business eight years later. Spadaro began wintering in Florida during the mid-1920s. In addition to being a concrete contractor, he was a developer and purchased property all over the west coast, from St. Petersburg and Tampa to Fort Myers, Boca Grande and Sarasota.

Spadaro's first project in Venice was a forty-unit rental complex called the Villas Apartments, built in four "U"-shaped, one-story solid concrete-walled buildings with red brick exterior, as well as a rental office building.

He completed the units in 1950 and included a yacht basin on the north side of the property. That same year, construction began on the Villas Hotel adjacent to the apartment complex and overlooking the beach. An article in the January 27, 1950 edition of the *Gondolier* described the building as a four-story structure offering 102 rooms of Spanish-type architecture and "will be laid out in the form of a giant cross." Spadaro added that work on the air-conditioned, fireproof complex would continue through the winter and summer so that the hotel would be ready for occupancy for the next tourist season. The hotel was later scaled back to a two-story building offering only 51 rooms.

Unfortunately, the Villas Hotel was not financially successful and eventually was replaced by the MacArthur Beach Hotel. That hotel, in turn, was replaced by the MacArthur Beach and Racquet Club. Villas Drive would become the northernmost boundary of the Golden Beach subdivision. The community is also bounded on the south and west by Golden Beach Boulevard and by Harbor Drive South on the east.

Following a year of illness and cancer, Joe Spadaro died on October 25, 1952. After his older brother's death, Anthony "Tony" Spadaro continued

MacArthur Beach Hotel, circa 1955. *Venice Historical Resources.*

Golden Beach, 1953. *Venice Historical Resources.*

many of the company's projects. He finished five homes on Spadaro Drive. They were all built on solid concrete bases raised above ground with solid concrete interior and exterior walls, faced in red brick, as Joe had designed them. Tony also began new construction projects, including a car wash at the intersection of U.S. 41 and San Marco Drive. He also built the gas station and diner located across the street and just north of the car wash.

In 1954, Tony and business partners Edward Darling, Robert Baynard and Orlando Mahon formed the AERO Corporation, the letters of their first names forming the company's name. They renamed the Villas subdivision Golden Beach in February 1954 when a new subdivision plat was filed with Sarasota County. Four streets in the new subdivision were named for the AERO officers. The company's founding also marked the end of buildings constructed to withstand the worst hurricanes. Many of the original homes were eventually replaced with larger, more modern homes.

In 1968, the Caspersen estate leased land to Sarasota County in exchange for waiving property taxes. The county would attempt to purchase the two-mile-long beachfront property, but negotiations became a little contentious when neither side could agree to a purchase price and the county threatened eminent domain. The county sold bonds to acquire several beachfront properties in Sarasota County, including the Caspersen land. It eventually acquired the property, and it became Caspersen Beach County Park.

While homes were springing up south of Venice, a new subdivision was emerging just north of the city. Bordering Roberts Bay, Bird Bay Village would become the area's first planned unit development.

When BLE Realty began building Venice in 1926, it hired noted landscape architect Prentiss French to design the city's natural beauty. Upon his arrival in January 1926, French set about creating a forty-acre nursey on the outskirts of the planned city. The location that would eventually become the site for Bird Bay was chosen for "its variety of soil, its proximity to the town, and its remoteness from possible development."

About a dozen nurserymen were operating the facility under the direction of F. Paul Horne, former superintendent of the New Orleans Park system. Horn was also responsible for previously landscaping John Ringling's estate in Sarasota. French imported thousands of plants and trees and kept them in stock at the nursery for planting.

Following the BLE Realty's abandonment of the Venice project, between 1926 and 1940, an orange grove of about twenty acres existed on the northeast corner of the property. After a misapplication of pesticide spray destroyed the trees, the grove was abandoned. Also, a three-hundred-acre dairy farm, owned by Cyrus Bispham of Sarasota, reportedly operated on the property.

The Bird Bay Realty Corporation was formed in 1955 with Howard W. Moore serving as president of Bird Bay Development. The area was rezoned from industrial to residential with the first plat approved by Sarasota County in 1957. The first lot was sold the following year.

Shortly before it dissolved in 1965, Bird Bay Realty would sell parcels totaling $156,000 to Venice attorney Gene Green. It was also about that time that construction of the U.S. 41 Bypass around Venice would take place. The bypass was part of the agreement reached in the spring of 1963 to complete the Intracoastal Waterway around Venice. The four-lane highway, opened in 1966 at a cost of more than $1 million, also bordered the southern end of the Bird Bay development.

In 1964, another national labor union came to Venice and took interest in the project. The Amalgamated Transit Union (ATU), based in Maryland and currently representing more than 200,000 members throughout the United States and Canada, saw the development as an opportunity for its retirees.

The ATU, along with the Crockett Mortgage Company, bought controlling interest in the Venice-Nokomis Bank. Three officers of the union would be elected to serve on the bank's board of directors. In 1966, the ATU also purchased $2.5 million worth of property from Green, which would be developed into two hundred small homes and complete a marina that had been started by Bird Bay Realty. The idea was that the union would sell the homes to retired union members at cost. The ATU, with Green serving as its attorney, petitioned the City of Venice in 1972 to annex the property into the city.

Although union officials had high hopes for its involvement in Bird Bay, the rank and file voted to abandon the project. In 1972, the Valencia Development Corporation acquired $780,000 worth of property from the ATU and sought further annexation of the property into the city. Once annexation was approved, Valencia began construction of the first "Sandpiper" section of condos in 1973. The company also began adding amenities such as indoor and outdoor heated pools, all-weather tennis courts, an eighteen-hole executive golf course and nature trails. One idea that was rejected was to build a cemetery on the site.

It was marketed as "the condominium with nature as a neighbor," and construction began in March 1973. A total of about 1,450 units was planned, consisting of one-, two- and three-bedroom garden apartments, town houses, villas and quadruplexes. Pre-construction prices began from $19,800. The Sandpiper section of homes opened in the fall of 1974, to be followed soon by the Cardinal, Laurel, Kingfisher and Seagrape sections.

Entrance to the sales showcase of Bird Bay at its grand opening, 1973. *Venice Historical Resources.*

Valencia Development opened a "Sales Showcase" on property adjacent to the bypass. In addition to the sales office, the complex included scaled-down models of the various units, as well as furnished apartment models. The sales complex set the stage for the later commercial development of the Bird Bay Shopping Center and the Bird Bay Plaza on the opposite side of the bypass. A traffic light, paid for by Valencia, was added to the intersection in 1975 to avoid traffic congestion. A total of 210 units was built before Valencia defaulted on its mortgage.

The Ramar Group, consisting of J.S. Carrion and Robert Morris, acquired the undeveloped property from the bank in 1977 for $3 million. Ramar continued to develop units and completed the once-promised recreation center. Ramar developed some of the last remaining properties along Curry Creek and Roberts Bay and constructed an 1,800-foot boardwalk along the shoreline in 1979 to better enjoy the flora and fauna. Acquiring the eighteen-hole executive golf course in the deal, it also worked with architect Ron Garl to upgrade the course, added a pro shop and hired Mike Toale as resident professional golfer. Bird Bay Village today consists of 1,026 condominium units, spread across 5.2 acres.

While the area experienced a building boom beginning in the 1950s, a new design known as the Sarasota School of Architecture also took the world by storm. A 1952 edition of *Architectural Review* proclaimed, "The most exciting new architecture in the world is being done in Sarasota by a group of young architects." The Sarasota School was never an organization. Rather, it was a collective of nearly two dozen architects who adhered to some unique design characteristics, such as rectangular, flat-roofed buildings with cantilevered overhangs that were narrow and designed with large planes of glass to optimize natural illumination and cross-ventilation. In the days before air conditioning became standard in residences, many were built with raised floors to avoid dampness and to foster natural cooling underneath. Their designs also featured local, natural materials utilizing new construction techniques. And new technologies were introduced such as jalousie windows, terrazzo floors and sliding glass doors that enhanced air flow.

The Sarasota School got its name based on a presentation by architect Gene Leedy at an American Institute of Architects Conference in 1982. "I was supposed to put on a big program about what we were doing, and I had to think of a name for the brochure," he would say later. "In those days, they used to refer to architects in Chicago as the 'Chicago School,' so I called us the 'Sarasota School' and it stuck."

Ralph Twitchell is considered the father of the Sarasota School. A student at Rollins College in Winter Park, he first visited the city in 1908 with a classmate who was from the area. After serving as a pilot in World War I, he studied engineering and architecture at Columbia University. He returned to Sarasota in 1925 to oversee construction of John Ringling's home, Cà d'Zan, on behalf of New York City architect Dwight James Baum. Twitchell established his own practice in Sarasota in 1936. He was largely influenced by famed architect Frank Lloyd Wright, who was designing many buildings at the time on the campus of Florida Southern College in nearby Lakeland. Twitchell also formed his own construction company, Associated Builders Inc., to assist his clients with the new construction materials and techniques. One of Twitchell's first projects was to design the home of actor and Pulitzer Prize–winning novelist MacKinlay Kantor. He went on to design numerous buildings along the Suncoast during his career, among them the iconic Lido Beach Casino in 1940. He designed several residences in Venice, including the Hudson Beach House in 1953 at 615 Valencia Road. He also designed in 1954 the beachfront home of Walter and Rosemary Farley in the Gulf Shores subdivision. Farley was the author of the "Black Stallion" book series, and the couple were instrumental in the founding of the Venice Library in 1965.

In 1941, a young draftsman named Paul Rudolf went to work for Twitchell. It was an ideal pairing, combining the Bauhaus and Organic approaches to architectural design, adapted for the Suncoast's warm and humid climate. If Twitchell is considered the father of the Sarasota School, Rudolf would have been its spiritual leader. Rudolf had recently graduated from Harvard's Graduate School of Design, where he studied under Walter Gropius, the founder of the Bauhaus School. He designed many notable buildings in Sarasota County, both with Twitchell and by his own practice, and went on to serve as the chairman of the Department of Architecture at Yale University from 1958 until 1965. He established his practice in New York City in 1966.

Another of Gropius's students at Harvard was Victor Lundy, who followed Rudolf to Sarasota in the early 1950s. His first project was to help the Venice-Nokomis Presbyterian Church, which, at the time, was operating a "drive-in" church with no buildings. He designed pro-bono a two-story wood and glass structure that enabled the pastor to be seen by the congregants as they worshiped amid the pine trees. *LIFE* magazine published a three-page article on the project in its April 18, 1955 edition, and a photograph of a family worshiping in their car featured Lundy and his family. Two years later, he

Venice-Nokomis Presbyterian Drive-In Church, circa 1954. *Venice Historical Resources.*

Sam Herron House, no date. *Venice Historical Resources.*

designed a fellowship hall for the church that eventually replaced the two-story structure. "My art form all my life has been architecture," Lundy said in a documentary about his work. "My strength is drawing. When I think thoughts, I draw thoughts."

Before moving his practice to New York City in 1960, Lundy designed several innovative buildings along the Suncoast. Perhaps the most iconic residence he designed in Venice was for local developer Sam Herron Jr. in 1957. Located at 615 Alhambra Road, the futuristic house is all curves and circles, with a soaring roof and big overhangs that create the impression it might fly away. The design won major awards and was featured in *LIFE*, *TIME* and *Look* magazines. Herron later hired Lundy to design his modernistic motel at Warm Mineral Springs.

As word spread about the movement, more young architects moved to the Suncoast, attracted by the innovative approaches taking place there. Other Sarasota School architects would later include Gene Leedy, Tim Seibert, Jack West, Bert Brosmith, Frank Folsom Smith and Carl Abbott. Although their architectural designs caught the attention of architects and admirers worldwide, the growing use of air conditioning, as well as the demand for cheaper and larger homes with less innovative architecture, led to a decline in the movement by the early 1960s. Many of the prominent architects like Rudolf, Lundy, Brosmith and Leedy moved their practices to larger metropolitan areas, where there was a greater demand for their services.

Ruth Richmond, no date. *Florida Memory.*

Many builders looked to emulate the Sarasota School style in Venice with cheaper and more modest homes. One example is Richmond Homes, particularly with Ruth Richmond. Ruth and her husband, Laurence, started their company in Tampa in 1950 and later moved to Sarasota. Over a span of twenty years, the company built more than twelve thousand homes in Southwest Florida. Quantity discounts lowered costs and allowed Ruth to design modest homes that paid homage to mid-century modern concepts. The business opened models throughout Sarasota County, including the 400 block of Barcelona Avenue in Venice, Venice Gardens, Venice East and eventually a "home center of ideas" at the corner of Business U.S. 41 and the U.S. 41 Bypass.

Ruth served as the designer for the business and is credited with introducing such innovations as Formica cabinets, sliding glass doors that disappeared behind walls and screen-enclosed porches, which she called lanais. Her custom-designed Lucite doorknobs and cabinet pulls have become collectors' items.

WHEN TERROR CAME TO TOWN

Three days before entering the new year and century, Venice citizens, employees and residents gathered in front of city hall to bury a twelve-cubic-inch waterproof vault filled with donated items for future generations to discover on January 1, 2100. Contained in the vault were copies of local newspapers and books on Venice history, as well as numerous personal contributions from residents of Venice.

"I hope the city is still around as a political jurisdiction in 100 years," said City Manager George Hunt, as reported in the January 1, 2001 edition of the *Venice Gondolier*. "Time capsules may be more appropriate in the future than they have been in the past because things are changing so rapidly." The mood was jubilant on that sunny winter Wednesday as the city of Venice, like the rest of the world, looked forward with expectation to the twenty-first century. Unbeknownst to residents was the knowledge that three Middle Eastern terrorists would soon slip into Venice to begin preparing for the most horrific and deadly attack to ever occur on American soil.

September 11, 2001, would become another day that would live in infamy. And the name of the little City on the Gulf would forever be associated with that tragedy. Marwan al-Shehhi, a Saudi, arrived in Venice from Germany in May 2000. Thirty-three-year-old Mohamed Atta of Egypt and Lebanese-born Ziad Jarrah arrived the following month. The fourth terrorist, who piloted the airliner into the Pentagon, would train in Arizona. Fourteen of the nineteen hijackers operated from Florida, and fifteen of the nineteen were of Saudi descent. In his book *Welcome to Terrorland*, author Daniel

A time capsule is placed outside city hall at the end of 1999, to be opened in 2100. *Venice Historical Resources.*

Hopsicker observed, "Florida is the biggest 9/11 crime scene that wasn't reduced to rubble." During the year and a half leading up to the attack, the Venice-based terrorists, like the rest, were moving around the state, as well as making short trips overseas. During the hours and days following that infamous morning, FBI agents swarmed all over the Sunshine State, and especially Venice, investigating clues and trying to piece together the timeline of events.

Atta and al-Shehhi signed up on July 6, 2000, for flying lessons at Venice-based Huffman Aviation. Atta spent roughly $18,000 for his lessons, while al-Shehhi spent an estimated $20,000. Why Venice? Rudi Dekkers, owner of Huffman Aviation, would later say that he recruited students from Europe because it was less expensive to learn to fly in Florida, largely because of the favorable weather. "It was cheaper to come here, stay here, get a license and return home than just learning to fly there," he told *Gondolier* reporter Bob Mudge.

During their time in Venice, the three pilots-in-training developed reputations among some locals. Jarrah, who reportedly left behind a girlfriend in Germany, maintained a low profile. Atta, on the other hand, was always well dressed and aloof, while al-Shehhi appeared more casual and more congenial. Some said that he created the impression of serving as

Huffman Aviation owner Rudy Dekkers answers questions about the two terrorists who trained at his flight school. *From the* Venice Gondolier.

Atta's bodyguard. One of the things that struck many about Atta was the dead look in his eyes and his unpleasant personality. Anne Graves, a fellow student of theirs at the training center, remembered, "It was just this sort of almost dead expression. Just no life in him whatsoever. Robotic. Not a flicker of emotion or excitement or anything. Nothing at all."

The terrorists rented a two-bedroom house in Nokomis. Atta, however, soon began a relationship with a young stripper who lived in a second-floor apartment directly across the street from the airport. Atta and al-Shehhi had rather unconventional habits for Muslims. They were known to frequent bars all over Florida, as well as a strip club in Sarasota called Cheetah's. There also was a time when the men and their lady friends spent a three-day alcohol and drug-induced binge in Key West. When Atta's girlfriend left him for another and left his bags outside her apartment, the terrorist left behind an example of his anger and psychotic behavior—he dismembered her cat and kittens and left body parts scattered throughout her apartment.

Atta and al-Shehhi obtained their multi-engine commercial pilot licenses from Huffman Aviation on December 21, 2000. They later attended a simulation training center in Opa-locka, Florida, where they spent two days training on a Boeing 727 full-motion flight simulator. They spent $1,500 in cash for the training. After that, there were numerous sightings of the men in Southeast Florida. Four days before the attacks, Atta was reportedly drinking heavily in a Hollywood, Florida bar and arguing over a $48 tab. Two days later, al-Shehhi checked out of a Deerfield Beach motel, along with another guest.

On that fateful Tuesday morning in September, Atta boarded American Airlines Flight 11 at Boston's Logan Airport, while al-Shehhi boarded United Airlines Flight 175 bound for Los Angeles. At 8:45 a.m., Atta's plane, with 92 souls aboard, slammed into the World Trade Center's north tower. Al-Shehhi's plane, with 65 souls aboard, crashed into the Center's south tower eighteen minutes later. Both towers had collapsed by 10:30 a.m. More than 2,900 died on that tragic day, including the 19 terrorists who committed murder-suicide. Dekker would later tell a reporter from *Good Morning America* that there were no clues that the two men who trained at Huffman Aviation had any agenda other than learning how to fly.

At the time of the attacks, President George W. Bush was in Sarasota, participating in an event at Booker Elementary School to promote his stand against illiteracy. He was in a second-grade classroom, listening to the

As Dan Bartlett, deputy assistant to the president, points to news footage of the World Trade Center, President George W. Bush gathers information about the terrorist attack from a classroom at Emma E. Booker Elementary School in Sarasota, Florida. Also pictured, *from left*, are Deborah Loewer, director of White House Situation Room, and Senior Adviser Karl Rove. *National Archives.*

students read, when an aide quietly informed him that planes had crashed into the World Trade Center. Bush was whisked to the local airport and flown to air force bases in Louisiana and Nebraska before determining that it was safe for him to return to D.C.

Michelle Miller and Tanya Poleschner, first-grade teachers at Laurel Nokomis School, told the *Sarasota Herald-Tribune* that they were in class when the attacks occurred. They learned of the event when a distraught parent stuck his head into Miller's classroom, related news of the bombings and removed his child. Eight more soon followed, while other parents pleaded with the teachers not to tell their children what was happening.

Venetians, like the rest of the world, were in shock as they learned of the attacks. The regularly scheduled city council meeting that afternoon was adjourned after only thirty-six minutes. "It's like we stepped into the 'Twilight Zone,'" said Venice Mayor Dean Calamaras. "All of a sudden, Venice is in the national news because of the terrorist connection. Then, the next day, I hear them talk about hurricanes crashing into the state at Venice. It's kind of surreal." Tropical storm Gabrielle swept ashore near Venice about 8:00 a.m. on Friday, September 14.

No one really learned about the city's connection to the terrorist attacks until the following Wednesday. On the evening of 9/11, Lieutenant Ron Solones was working the midnight shift at the Venice Police Department when he intercepted an FBI message asking for any information on one of the cars used by the hijackers. When he ran the license plate number, it connected with a South Venice address.

By Wednesday morning, Venice was inundated with FBI agents, national media and others seeking to understand the city's connection to the terrorist attack. Mike Pachota, owner of Sharkey's Restaurant on the Pier, told a *Sarasota Herald-Tribune* reporter that it was "just amazing that here in our little town…there would be even remotely a piece of the puzzle that fits into the whole scheme of things."

In the following days, the shock over the city's involvement transformed into the awareness of Venice's vulnerability to any future attacks. A chain link and barbed wire fence was installed around Venice's water plant, complete with twenty-four-hour armed guards, to protect against any attempts to poison the water supply. The bay doors that usually remained open at the fire station were left closed to prevent the theft of any dangerous chemicals. And the ability to just walk into city hall unannounced was no longer an option.

Venice Police Sergeant Tom McNulty, *left*, and FBI agent Kelly Thomas haul files from Huffman Aviation at Venice Municipal Airport shortly after the September 11 terrorist attack. *From the* Venice Gondolier.

Reverend J.C. Sims stands behind a fence that was erected around his church after the September 11 attacks. The City of Venice put up the fence to protect the water plant that is located next to the church. *From the* Sarasota Herald-Tribune.

Ruminating on whether Venice's connection to the terrorists would leave any long-lasting stain on the city's reputation, Venice Vice Mayor Jim Myers told a *Sarasota Herald-Tribune* reporter, "It certainly awakened a lot of people to the fact you never know where terrorists might be doing their thing."

While the initial shock of the attack may fade in time, most will remember those whose lives were lost on that fateful day. At the May 28, 2002 meeting of the city council, Mayor Calamaras announced that Patriot Park, located on the city's north side, would honor "all who have served in the armed forces and those who lost their lives in the 9/11 attack." The site of annual gatherings on Memorial Day, 9/11 and other special occasions, Patriot Park contains a two-ton steel beam from the World Trade South Tower, with the names of all those who died on 9/11 etched in the base.

VENICE IN THE TWENTY-FIRST CENTURY

Venice spent the first half of its existence wondering if there were sufficient resources for the city to survive. By the twenty-first century, that narrative had flipped. Many residents became increasingly concerned that perhaps too much of a good thing had overtaken their city on the Gulf, threatening the very quality of life that drew settlers to the Suncoast in the first place.

City leaders over the years continued to embrace John Nolen's plan for designing Venice. And because there was not a great demand for the property, many of the more than one hundred residences and retail buildings constructed in the mid-1920s were not destroyed. As a result, Venice remained one of the finest examples of the garden-city movement that continued to flourish until World War II. Modern city planners continue to study Nolen's walkable design for Venice. In addition to four separate National Historic Districts within the city, John Nolen's plan for Venice was added as the fifth to the National Register of Historic Places in 2010.

With the new millennium and the increasing migration of wealthy retirees toward warmer climates, Venice continued to grow and expand. The population reached 17,764 residents in 2000, an increase of 5 percent over the previous decade. And because the heart of Venice was now located on a man-made island created by the Intracoastal Waterway (ICW)—serving as somewhat of a barrier against urban sprawl—rapid growth continued well beyond its traditional borders.

Following a lengthy, sometimes raucous debate, including a petition from residents to put the issue up for a general vote, the Venice City Council in February 2000 approved annexing the 1,100-acre Henry Ranch into the city. The property, located north of Laurel Road and east of I-75, would eventually be developed by Watermark Communities as the Venetian Golf & River Club. It would offer nearly 1,600 single-family homes plus golf and tennis facilities. Adjacent to the Myakka River, the developer also planned for a 10-acre park on the property. The annexation opened the door for further expansion throughout the Northeast corridor, as well as much of the former Venice Farms area east of town. And while developers were not opposed to many of the principles set forth by Nolen and other city planners of that time, what modern home buyers wanted were suburban-style gated communities. By 2024, there were twenty-seven gated communities in Venice.

As Pat Neal, one of the more prolific developers in South Sarasota County, told a reporter in the March 3, 2021 edition of *Sarasota Magazine*, "In Nolen's time, the automobile had not begun to dominate American residential planning. Everything had to be walkable. Now, overwhelmingly, the market prefers 21st-century building." He continued, "New urbanism is cute and builds community and has its place, and we'd build more of it if we saw a market for it."

Unbridled growth was a concern for Venetians as much as for communities all over Florida. The Florida legislature in 1985 established the Growth Management Act, which required all local governments to adopt comprehensive land use plans aligned with state guidelines. By the mid-2000s, the City of Venice had begun a comprehensive citizen-based planning process called "Envision Venice" that would provide long-range planning for the city. The project addressed several aspects of future life in Venice. Everyone agreed that the ultimate mission of the plan was to maintain Venice as a vibrant, charming, historic community in which to live, work and play.

The community worked toward accomplishing some of the goals outlined in that comprehensive plan. But the city also struggled with numerous setbacks, such as the economic recession in 2008. Florida lost 10 percent of its economy during the worst of the downturn, ranking the state forty-eighth compared to declines in other states. The June 9, 2010 edition of the *Venice Gondolier* announced that the Holiday Inn Express, located near I-75, was the fourth Venice hotel to foreclose in the previous ten months. Many more businesses and residences with adjustable-rate mortgages were also forced into foreclosure.

The Venetian Waterway Trail along the ICW. *Venice Area Beautification.*

One month later, City Manager Isaac Turner was forced to lay off four experienced city workers, with more layoffs likely he said, based on a draft of the 2010–11 city budget. "With 76.7 percent of the general fund going toward salaries and benefits for employees, it is inevitable that substantial expenditure reductions will necessitate reduction in the number of employee positions," he stated in his budget transmittal letter.

By 2018, as Venice continued to rebound from the recession, an unprecedented red tide bloom decimated local marine life and affected the health and economy of the city, which depended largely on tourism for its livelihood. Two years later, Venice faced the worldwide COVID pandemic.

Despite the obstacles, Venice and surrounding areas continued to grow in numbers. And residents continued to discover the benefits of life on the Suncoast, including amenities created by public-private partnerships. For example, a collaboration between the City of Venice, Sarasota County and Venice Area Beautification Inc. (VABI) created the Venetian Waterway Trail Park, which offers some ten miles of concrete bike trails along both sides of the ICW that passes through Venice. The trail also connects with the Legacy Trail, which opened in 2008 and provides more than twenty miles of rail trails connecting Venice with both Sarasota to the north and North Port and beyond to the south.

The Venice Little Theatre acquired the former KMI gymnasium for its new home in 1973. *Venice Historical Resources.*

In 2018, VABI volunteers began efforts to turn the twenty-six acres of land on the east side of the ICW, and in the heart of the city, into an Urban Forest. The forest aligns with John Nolen's City Garden plan with nature running through the heart of the city. VABI volunteers also spend countless hours maintaining lush landscapes throughout the city's historic downtown, continually earning Venice recognition as one of America's most beautiful cities.

To remain sustainable, Venice continues to encourage and support local businesses that contribute to the local economy. Companies like PGT and Tervis, which got their start in Venice decades ago, have continued to flourish. Local business growth is supported by organizations such as the Venice Area Chamber of Commerce and Venice MainStreet, which is committed to preserving and enhancing the vitality of the city's historic downtown.

Venice has a homogeneous population. In 2021, the city reported a population of about twenty-five thousand residents, with a median age of 68.6; more than 90 percent of respondents listing themselves as white (Non-Hispanic). The median household income was $65,478. The median property value was $290,600, and the homeownership rate was 79.6 percent.

As Venice continues to grow in the twenty-first century, local arts organizations are expanding to meet the demands of those increasing residents as well. The Venice Theatre, for example, which traces its roots back to 1950 and an old Quonset hut on the former army base, is now ranked as the third-largest community theater in America and the largest per capita. By 2006, attendance reached 85,000, supported by more than 1,200 volunteers. In September 2022, Hurricane Ian destroyed the roof covering the main stage area. Work on the repairs, estimated to cost more than $14 million, began almost immediately while smaller performances continued in the Raymond Center and on the Pinkerton Stage.

Other cultural organizations continued to expand their outreach in the twenty-first century as well. The Venice Performing Arts Center (VPAC) is located adjacent to Venice High School and is owned by the Sarasota County School Board. Formally opened on November 6, 2014, the facility seats 1,090 people and hosts several local arts organizations, including the Venice Symphony, the Venice Chorale and the Venice Concert Band. The Center also hosts dozens of high school events annually and provides students with a pre-professional program where they receive career-ready skills in the performing arts.

In 1968, the city allowed the Venice Art League to build a 5,000-square-foot Art Center in East Blalock Park and provided the group with a ninety-nine-year lease at the rate of one dollar per year. It completed a 4,000-square-foot addition around 1997. By 2018, the Venice Art Center boasted more than 1,400 members and about 260 volunteers. Located just north of the art center is the Dr. William H. Jervey Jr. Venice Public Library, which was completed in 2019. The 19,428-square-foot facility provides multimedia resources as well as an auditorium and meeting rooms for public use.

Venice Area Art League before it expanded to become the Venice Art Center, circa 1979. *Venice Historical Resources.*

The Triangle Inn was relocated to save it from demolition. It would become the Venice Museum. *Venice Historical Resources.*

Also located in what has come to be called Venice's Cultural Campus is the Triangle Inn, which houses the city's history museum. When the 1927 boardinghouse was threatened with demolition in November 1991, city leaders agreed to acquire and move it two blocks south to its present location. With the creation of the nonprofit Triangle Inn Association, along with grants and donations, the building became home to the city's museum in 1996. The building, along with the Julia Cousins Laning and Dale Laning Archives & Research Center, is maintained by the city's Division of Historical Resources.

A good PR man in 1926 described Venice as "the new 'Resort Supreme' of Florida's West Coast Riviera." The burgeoning city offered the hope of an idyllic, walkable community in which one could live, work and play. During the next one hundred years, the question for future leaders will be whether Venice can continue to progress and evolve with one foot firmly planted in its rich, historic past.

BIBLIOGRAPHY

Albee, Fred H. *A Surgeon's Fight to Rebuild Men*. E.P. Dutton & Company, 1943.

Albee, Louella. *Doctor and I*. S.J. Bloch Publishing Company, 1951.

Cassell, Frank. *Creating Sarasota County*. The History Press, 2019.

———. *Suncoast Empire*. Pineapple Press, 2017.

Character Makes the Man: The Story of the Kentucky Military Institute, 1845–1971. KMI Alumni Association, 2014.

Cool, Kim. *Circus Days in Sarasota and Venice*. Historic Venice Press, 2004.

Ennes, Stanton. "The Locomotive Engineers Investment in Florida Real Estate, Venice." *Sarasota Times*, 1929.

Foster, William Z. *Wrecking the Labor Banks: The Collapse of the Labor Banks and Investment Companies of the Brotherhood of Locomotive Engineers*. Trade Union Educational League, 1927.

Hackett, Kim. "From New Urbanism to Suburbanism, Venice Is a Tale of Two Cities." *Sarasota Magazine* (2021).

Harner, Charles. *Florida's Promoters: The Men Who Made It Big*. Trend House, 1973.

Hillman, Sidney. *The Labor Banking Movement in the United States*. Proceedings of the Academy of Political Science in the City of New York, April 1925, 109–18.

Korwek, Dorothy, and Carl Shiver. *John Nolen Plan of Venice, Florida*. Triangle Inn Association, 2011.

LaHurd, Jeff. *Hidden History of Sarasota*. The History Press, 2009.

Matthews, Janet Snyder. *Venice: Journey from Horse and Chaise: A History of Venice, Florida*. Pine Level Press, 1989.

Pressly, Clarke. *The First Mayor of Venice: Edward L "Ned" Worthington*. Venice Area Historical Society, 2021.

Sarasota Times. 1910–2023.

Stephenson, R. Bruce. *John Nolen, Landscape Architect and City Planner*. University of Massachusetts Press, in association with Library of American Landscape History, 2015.

Thole, Lou. *Forgotten Fields of America*. Pictorial Histories Publishing Company, 2003.

Turner, Gregg M. *Venice in the 1920s*. Arcadia Publishing, 2000.

Van Fleet, Frederick A. *A Disaster in Management*. Nation's Business, 1929.

Venice (FL) Gondolier. 1946–2023.

Wimmers, H.N. Audiotaped interview conducted on July 3, 1975, by Hack Swain Productions.

Youngberg, George E., Sr., and W. Earl Aumann. *Venice and the Venice Area*. Venice Area Historical Society, 2008.

ABOUT THE AUTHOR

During his four-decade-long career, Larry R. Humes worked mostly in journalism and higher education marketing and communication. He wrote for newspapers throughout Florida, served as a stringer for United Press International and was editor of the *Greentree Gazette*, a bimonthly national magazine targeting higher education administrators. His mystery novel *Bridge to Nowhere* was published in 1980. Larry managed communications for the University of Florida and Rollins College before spending the last decade of his career as a strategic marketing and communications consultant to higher education. Since retirement, he has remained active in local history projects and gives presentations on the topic. He also writes regularly about local history for the *Venice Gondolier* newspaper. He can be reached at 1926venice@gmail.com.

Visit us at
www.historypress.com
....